True organizational excellence, in healthcare and every other industry, requires much more than just a set of tools. It requires the right behaviors guided by the right principles. *Becoming the Change* teaches leaders what behaviors they need to adopt to change their healthcare organizations and set them on a path of excellence. This book provides excellent case studies from which all healthcare professionals can benefit. I encourage all to take these lessons to heart and *be* the change.

—Ken Snyder
Executive Director, Shingo Institute,
Utah State University

With this book, Toussaint and Barnas address the elephant in the room by calling for a radically new way of leading our nation's healthcare organizations. They aim to start nothing short of a revolution. Do you lead with humility, ask a lot of questions, not pretend to have the answers, and create an organization where everyone is a problem solver? If not, you read this book at your peril. You are being asked to change a large part of who you are.

—Stephen M. Shortell, PhD, MPH, MBA
Distinguished Professor of Health Policy and
Management Emeritus, Dean Emeritus, and
Co-Director of the Center for Lean Engagement
and Research (CLEAR) in Healthcare,
School of Public Health, UC Berkeley

Becoming the Change provides much needed practical advice to healthcare leaders at all levels on both the reflection and actions required to change their leadership behaviors. The book is filled with examples throughout and provides a template for a personal A3 that guides the leader through his or her leadership transformation. Written by two accomplished leaders in healthcare improvement, the book is a compelling read that fills a real development need from the board of directors to the front line.

—Peter Ward
Richard M. Ross Chair in Management and
Director of the Center for Operational
Excellence, The Ohio State University

Supported by strong field research and evidence from several healthcare systems, this book offers great insights. It is a playbook for every healthcare leader at various phases in their lean journey.

—Aravind Chandrasekaran
Professor of Operations,
The Ohio State University

Becoming
the Change

Becoming
the Change

Leadership Behavior Strategies for
Continuous Improvement in Healthcare

John Toussaint, MD | **Kim Barnas**
with Emily Adams

New York   Chicago   San Francisco   Athens   London   Madrid
Mexico City   Milan   New Delhi   Singapore   Sydney   Toronto

1 2 3 4 5 6 7 8 9   LCR   25 24 23 22 21 20

ISBN   978-1-260-46168-8
MHID   1-260-46168-8

e-ISBN   978-1-260-46169-5
e-MHID   1-260-46169-6

Library of Congress Cataloging-in-Publication Data

Names: Toussaint, John, author. | Barnas, Kim, author. | Adams, Emily, contributor.
Title: Becoming the change : leadership behavior strategies for continuous improvement in healthcare / John Toussaint, MD, and Kim Barnas; with Emily Adams.
Description: New York : McGraw-Hill, [2020] | Includes bibliographical references and index.
Identifiers: LCCN 2020014191 (print) | LCCN 2020014192 (ebook) | ISBN 9781260461688 (hardback) | ISBN 9781260461695 (ebook)
Subjects: LCSH: Health services administration. | Organizational change. | Leadership.
Classification: LCC RA971 .T678 2020 (print) | LCC RA971 (ebook) | DDC 362.1068—dc23
LC record available at https://lccn.loc.gov/2020014191
LC ebook record available at https://lccn.loc.gov/2020014192

*To the courageous healthcare leaders who are changing
the face of healthcare delivery across the globe:
the tales we tell are meant to inspire and provide
hope that no matter what the circumstances, leaders
who begin to act differently improve lives and
sometimes save the lives of the people they serve.*

CONTENTS

PART III
Opportunities

PREFACE

We were in the final stages of completing this manuscript when Covid-19 became an international pandemic, upending lives around the globe, creating heroes out of healthcare workers everywhere. Physicians and nurses came out of retirement in New York; obstetricians in Wisconsin scrounged up protective gear to help in the intensive care units (ICUs). Family doctors staffed rapidly constructed respiratory centers, and every evening in major cities around the world, people went out on their balconies and cheered for the healthcare workers who were risking their lives to save us.

What do we owe them, those frontline caregivers who donned hazmat suits and reused N-95 masks and dragged themselves to the emergency room for another 16-hour shift, day after night? Certainly, we have all learned the importance of keeping an adequate supply of personal protective equipment (PPE). We know now, with the clarity of a slap in the face, the problems inherent in the for-profit supply lines that surround our nonprofit hospitals. Some of these issues will need to be corrected at the national level.

On a local level, we saw that some hospitals and health systems responded to the challenges better than others. At Duke University in North Carolina, research and clinical teams developed and tested a new way to disinfect masks with hydrogen peroxide to allow safe reuse. They quickly obtained FDA approval and shared the procedure with the world.

At Morningside Mt. Sinai in New York, leaders created a digital dashboard that displayed real-time information for both clinical and nonclinical operations. Using the structure of their management system and multiple daily team huddles, they quickly had a system in place to collect and share critical information with all, such as:

1. Total number of Covid-19 patients and their bed locations (ICU, non-ICU, ED) and total number of persons under investigation (PUI) and their locations
2. Total number of Covid-19 and PUI patient deaths
3. Total transfers from ICU to non-ICU and vice versa; total number of patients on invasive and noninvasive ventilation

Creative solutions like collecting $1 plastic ponchos from sporting arenas for use during intubation and splitting ventilator tubing to accommodate two to four patients at a time came from organizations focused on safety, communication, and frontline problem solving to support caregivers.

It requires leadership resolve to create and support good systems. Work groups that convene to better understand and address gaps between needs and reality, and consistent team huddles to move information up and down the line, do not happen without executive support.

Some hospitals have had a more difficult time. Leaders who fell back on command-and-control instincts found themselves in charge of every answer, every emerging issue—an unsustainable position in a long fight and one that failed to offer adequate support for exhausted staff. It was heartbreaking to see hospitals rely on the heroic efforts of the front line.

A lot will be changing for healthcare in the months and years ahead. Supply chains will be fundamentally reshaped.

Caregivers will be paying close attention to how they and their families will be protected during the next global pandemic. Good leaders—who looked at the yawning gaps in their care systems and realized that they alone could not fill them—will be demanding better resources.

While we celebrate heroes, we cannot demand this of our people. We cannot ask them to put themselves in harm's way unless we are willing to work alongside them, improving their ability to provide care while keeping themselves safe. This book is about the efforts of healthcare organizations around the world to do just that. It is about leaders who are confronting their own gaps and undergoing personal change in order to better support the front line. We cannot imagine a more important message at this critical juncture.

We dedicate this book to all of the courageous healthcare workers and leaders who have been risking their lives daily to trounce this pandemic. We salute you. We admire you, and we hope this book will inspire you to persevere in your efforts to improve the human condition.

INTRODUCTION

The Current State of Healthcare

Healthcare is in the midst of a massive disruption. Financial structures are in tatters. Public trust is shaky. Every aspect of the way we care for people is up for reconsideration, and, if we take advantage of this moment, we can create a better system. Imagine the changes we are capable of: Avoidable mortality and hospital-acquired infections could plummet in the coming months, while patient satisfaction rates climb. Waste in the system can drop by double-digit percentage points.

Does this sound like a fantasy? A nationwide survey of healthcare organizations conducted by UC Berkeley in 2017 found that nearly 70 percent of healthcare systems were actively engaged in improvement initiatives such as lean thinking, organizational excellence, or Lean Six Sigma.[1] Seventy percent.

Most health systems were still in the early stages of these initiatives. Those with more mature initiatives—including a daily management system, widespread education, and leadership involvement—were reporting substantial improvement. The more mature the effort, the better the results.

The tide is starting to turn. The question is, can healthcare providers keep at it, creating enough improvement momentum to make this vision of a quality revolution come true?

---

1. Stephen M. Shortell, James C. Blodgett, Thomas G. Rundall, and Peter Kralovec, "Use of Lean and Related Transformational Performance Improvement Systems in Hospitals in the United States: Results from a National Survey," *The Joint Commission Journal on Quality and Patient Safety* 44, no. 10 (October 2018): 574–582.

We want to be optimistic. After more than a decade of executive coaching, teaching improvement methods through our not-for-profit, peer-to-peer learning center, and being inside hospitals in 19 countries where we have had the privilege of seeing hundreds of healthcare improvement initiatives in practice, we can say there is reason for optimism. After all, 70 percent of hospitals in the United States are putting serious effort into making positive change.

But only 12.6 percent of those hospitals report having a mature initiative with a daily management system[2] and leadership involvement. We know from long experience that a whole-health-system effort is necessary to create sustainable improvement. The majority of health systems, however, have efforts that are confined to one or two departments or clinics—usually the Emergency Department (ED), Surgery, or Labor and Delivery—and too many leaders seem content to keep improvement quarantined this way.

In those hospitals where the work is isolated, improvement is slowly crumbling all the time. Newly transformed departments are held together by occasional heroics and the sheer determination of people who have seen that the new way is better for patients.

Leaders, meanwhile, are in their offices and conference rooms, leading their organizations exactly as they led them before: full of answers and directives, yet disassociated from the work. What we have witnessed in hundreds of hospitals and health systems is that autocracy and improvement initiatives do not mix well. The signs of disengaged or autocratic leaders are improved

---

2. In its simplest definition, a daily management system uncovers frontline problems and potential problems in a daily series of one-on-one status exchanges and team huddles, creating a clear path to escalate problems up the chain of command when necessary, and provides leaders with ways to communicate strategy to all and ensure that mission-critical projects and concerns are addressed in the course of daily business.

departments—an exceptional cath lab, a NICU that exceeds everyone's goals—that are allowed to exist as islands of excellence. Or it might be frontline improvement work across several departments that never affects the working habits or expectations of executives in charge. Those leaders might brag about improved metrics, but they do not invite change into their own offices.

This situation has created the biggest gap between intention and execution that we have seen in organizations struggling to transform. Most often, leaders are not even aware that they are the roadblocks to reform.

This book exists because we have seen organizations correct course and have their improvement efforts take off with renewed vigor. In every case, the solution involved people making the conscious decision to change their leadership styles, altering the way they work and how they talk to peers, direct reports, and people on the front line.

We have seen that when leaders embrace new behaviors that are firmly based in commonly shared principles such as humility and respect for every person, improvement initiatives thrive. When leadership teams deliberately change their communication styles in support of an improvement initiative, the effects are fast and profound. One health system in Great Britain went from being ranked in the bottom third of the national health system to achieving top-third ratings in 18 months. In South Africa, another organization reduced infant mortality by 75 percent and maternal mortality by 40 percent in a single year. And in 2019, the orthopedic ICU's hospital-acquired infection rate dropped from 12 percent to 1 percent in nine months.

These are organizations run by leaders who know they cannot succeed by pushing new work processes at frontline caregivers. These are leaders who have embodied the transformation by adopting change at a personal level.

Through illustrations and outcomes data in this book, we can prove that this change in leadership behavior is necessary for improvement initiatives to survive and that leaders—executives, managers, and governance board members alike—therefore have direct impact on the health of patients.

Before we begin making our case for this change at a personal level, however, we need to examine the current condition of improvement efforts in healthcare. This is what we always do: examine what *is* before moving on to what should be.

It may be difficult for some to remember, but there was a time just before the turn of the century that Americans took it on faith that people in the United States enjoyed the best healthcare on the planet. Every advance in medicine, every foreign dignitary who came to the United States for complicated medical treatment, was proof of our standing in the world. Even as medical insurance prices skyrocketed and car manufacturers complained that employee health insurance cost more on a per-car basis than steel, we believed that, anyway, we were paying for the very best care.

And then in November 1999, the Institute of Medicine put out a report estimating that as many as 98,000 people per year were dying due to medical error.[3] The report was seized on by the media. Soon, every research project that showed quality problems in healthcare—from outright negligence to inaccuracies in recording prescription information—was given headlines in newspapers, documentaries, and broadcast news. This was a necessary eye-opener for all of healthcare.

When studies from Dartmouth University's Atlas Project then started to reveal the inequities in how medical resources

---

3. L. T. Kohn, J. Corrigan, and M. S. Donaldson, eds., *To Err Is Human: Building a Safer Health System* (Washington, D.C.: National Academy Press, 2000).

are distributed and used in this country—and the enormous variables in cost for the same care from one town to the next—it underlined the fact that our healthcare system was broken.[4]

And it was not just the United States that had problems. European countries, African countries, and other countries in the Americas started openly discussing their healthcare quality issues, too. Whether the systems were market-driven or nationalized did not matter. It was not the source of funding; it was how care was delivered.

FINDING THE FIX?

In the first decade of this century, many healthcare organizations around the country vowed to find a fix. None of us—physicians, nurses, administrators—wanted to work in a hospital where patient harm was acceptable. But how were we supposed to start fixing it? Those of us who recognized our problems also saw they were deeply rooted.

We looked for answers in new places, such as manufacturing companies that had been improving quality and reducing waste with ideas from the Toyota Production System. As the CEO (John) and president of hospitals (Kim) of a major not-for-profit, cradle-to-grave health system in Wisconsin, we learned about these methods up close as we embraced what was known as lean thinking. We led different pieces of the initiative, and we both saw wild successes.

Beginning in 2002, teams throughout our organization applied the tools and ideas we learned and reduced, for instance, our cardiac mortality to near zero. We reduced patient time in

---

4. www.dartmouthatlas.org.

hospital beds, improved their health outcomes, and—just in the first three years—cut costs by $27 million. We passed those savings along and became the lowest-price healthcare provider in the state.[5]

We were not the only ones. By 2015, it was common to hear hospital leaders around the country talk about their newly "lean" emergency rooms with strikingly low patient wait times. Major health systems in Seattle, Boston, Denver, and New York were trumpeting their patient safety records, the elimination of certain hospital-acquired infections, and their patient satisfaction scores.

But there was a dark side to all this accomplishment. Teaching lean or Toyota methods to health systems had become a cottage industry. Lean consultants who sold their services to healthcare had a standard playbook. They came into hospitals looking for the obvious signs of waste, otherwise known as low-hanging fruit, and then taught a team of employees the necessary tools to correct the situation.

Then the consultant added up the savings, presented the findings to leadership—almost always showing that the savings were greater than the consulting bill—and booked more work. Certain kinds of "transformation" rushed through our industry like fads, such as those super-efficient EDs and faster door-to-balloon cardiac surgeries.[6] A team would learn the tools and ideas to transform an area, write about their success in a journal or share it at a conference, and others would copy it. New work processes spread quickly.

---

5. John Toussaint and Roger A. Gerard, *On the Mend: Revolutionizing Healthcare to Save Lives and Transform the Industry* (Lean Enterprise Institute: 2010).

6. Door-to-balloon time is a measure of how quickly an arriving cardiac patient made it from the front door to the cardiac catheterization lab for treatment.

What we did not really understand was how much we were losing with each iteration of a solution. The teams doing the first transformation work in an organization were taught the value and purpose of a customer-centric value stream. Team members deconstructed and constructed working processes and deeply understood the needs of people working in an area.

But then, that team's solution was too often applied to new areas or different hospitals or clinics without transferring the knowledge. If people in the new area did not understand why work was organized in this way or have an opportunity to work through their own problems, they just felt imposed upon.

There was another problem, too. Even those initial improvement projects—where everyone was trained and fully engaged in the transformation—usually began to see erosion in improvement scores after a few months. Islands of excellence often appeared to plateau or sink over time. People at the front line and their immediate managers stressed over the seeming failures and were unsure how to lead through change. And these setbacks proved to be a bigger problem than they might be in other industries.

The front line of healthcare is made up of highly trained experts with an emotional stake in the outcome of their work. People live or die at our hands. We do not want to claim healthcare exceptionalism across the board, but there are qualitative differences between caring for humans and building machines. That first wave of consultants—who usually began their careers as manufacturing engineers—did not always understand this. Too many times people at the front line felt pushed around by engineers coming in and telling them how to do their work or what was important. And if the improvements fell apart, caregivers took it personally. They became less willing to put in time and effort on the next attempt.

Healthcare executives, meanwhile, were often told that if they just committed to a regular schedule of *kaizen*,[7] celebrated the work, and knocked down barriers that got in a team's way, their job as a lean leader was done.

Those of us who were very interested in the work also went to *gemba*[8] regularly, practiced asking open-ended questions, and learned how to coach people to solve their own problems. Even that was not enough.

LOOKING PAST THE FRONT LINE

In our Wisconsin health system, Kim saw the problems with sustaining improvement as a management gap. She put together a team and created a much-needed daily management system that worked with, instead of against, the team-based improvement work.[9] John became CEO emeritus and founded an organization, Catalysis, to help others learn these methods. He created a kind of transformational road map[10] and studied improvement systems around the globe, looking for answers from failures as well as successes. Kim joined Catalysis in 2014 and began to see the same problems as John.

What became most clear to us during this time was that CEOs and executive teams were disconnected from

---

7. *Kaizen* is from the Japanese symbols meaning *change* and *good*. It is translated as *change for the better* and often refers to a lean improvement project in which a cross-functional team studies and then improves an area or process in one week.

8. *Gemba* is a Japanese word popularized by the Toyota Production System; it means the place where real value is created. In a hospital, gemba is located wherever caregivers are directly helping patients.

9. Kim Barnas, *Beyond Heroes: A Lean Management System for Healthcare* (Theda-Care Center for Healthcare Value, 2014).

10. John Toussaint, *Management on the Mend: The Healthcare Executive Guide to System Transformation* (ThedaCare Center for Healthcare Value, 2015).

improvement work at the front line. Furthermore, their bosses—governing board members—were often not even aware that anything different was required of leaders in a lean organization. Executives were being judged by profit and loss statements. Managers were being judged by their ability to maintain control. And the frontline caregivers—who were too often introduced to lean thinking by consultants looking for redundancies in the process so that everyone could do more with less—were saying that lean was mean.

It turns out that lean *was* mean, largely because dramatic changes required by lean thinking were directed at some people instead of being adopted by all the people. *Lean* became so closely associated with *mean* in healthcare, the term *lean* became a liability.

Just to be clear: almost all of the improvement initiatives being used in healthcare in the aughts and teens of the twenty-first century stem from the same place, no matter the name. Whether it was called lean thinking or Lean Sigma or robust process improvement, it was all based in the twentieth-century ideas and teaching of statistician, professor, and management consultant W. Edwards Deming. Deming was the first person to identify the principles of a management philosophy guiding organizational excellence that was different from what American companies were practicing in the forties and fifties. Toyota, around the same time, established a set of guiding principles that became the Toyota Production System, which was translated back into North American English in the 1980s by James Womack and John Shook.

These initiatives focused on removing waste from processes, searching for problems instead of covering them up, using the plan-do-study-act (PDSA) cycle to address those problems, organizing work in value streams focused on the customer instead of internal needs, standardizing work, and using team-based problem solving.[11]

And that list, we finally came to realize, was a big part of the problem. Improvement work was consistently described this way: a set of tools, a way to look at resources, a restructuring of work processes. Improvement was made up of big external gestures that created redesigned hospital wings.

But what we have discovered is that the most important part of this work is internal. It is personal. Beginning with executives and board members, leaders in an organization that seek transformation must change how they behave toward other people. The way we think and ask about problems, how we define our roles, and how we gauge success are all up for renewal.

We know this is true because every time we examined an organization that was having trouble sustaining its improvement efforts, we found executives stuck in command-and-control style management. And every time we found an organization that was spreading its improvement work past the model cell[12] and finding new solutions, there were leaders who displayed humility, curiosity, self-discipline, and other traits that were crucial to their effort. These leaders were not magical beings; they were usually not born this way. These were leaders who adopted these traits because that is what they decided was best for the organization.

---

11. This is, essentially, a beefed-up version of the scientific method: developing a hypothesis based upon a study of current conditions, carrying out an experiment, analyzing the results of that experiment, and acting on that information with implementation of a new hypothesis.

12. A model cell pertains to any clinical or administrative department with identified business problems, such as throughput, quality, patient satisfaction, or cost, that are critical to the organization's mission and future. This is where a cross-functional frontline team redesigns work processes, with active support from top management, to achieve big—50 to 100 percent—improvements.

As we searched for a way to organize our thinking around the best leadership behaviors we were seeing, we kept returning to the list of guiding principles written by the Shingo Institute at Utah State University:

- Respect every individual.
- Lead with humility.
- Seek perfection.
- Embrace scientific thinking.
- Focus on process.
- Assure quality at the source.
- Flow and pull value.
- Think systemically.
- Maintain constancy of purpose.
- Create value for the customer.

In that list, we found all the bedrock principles that the best organizations were using—consciously or not—to define the traits and behaviors that were required of leaders. Working with these organizations, many of whom will be profiled in these pages, we further defined these principle-driven traits: willingness to change, leading with humility, curiosity, perseverance, and self-discipline.

Nobody perfectly embodied these principles and traits all the time. One executive might be naturally humble, but really needed to work at displaying self-discipline to the team. Another leader was good at staying on-topic and was entirely reliable, but still wanted to blurt out "the answer" to a problem.

The leadership teams that were most successful at supporting improvement work decided together on the most important principles and traits to embody and then held each other responsible. They worked at improving their behaviors. When people stumbled, they could expect a gentle correction from team members.

Because we know now that revolutionary change requires both internal and external transformation, when we need to label our methodology, we usually talk about *organizational excellence* instead of lean. It is a bigger tent of a label, and it reflects our more holistic approach.

When asked to help a struggling organization, we now begin with a full system assessment—from the internal drivers and behaviors of the executive team to how problems are uncovered and solved at the front line. It turns out that all of this matters. Readers will be able to perform their own assessments in Chapter 7.

Based on the assessments, leadership teams then agree upon organizational principles, establish the most important traits and behaviors for their team, and decide how they will hold each other accountable.

The most common traits required for people at each level of an organization are illustrated in Chapters 3 through 7. Since all traits are based in an organization's principles, it is impossible to say exactly which ones are required for every level of leadership in every health system. But there are strong commonalities from one organization to the next in what is required to support the work.

In general, top leaders need to get out of their offices. They need to listen rather than talk, to learn how to ask good questions, and to become vulnerable with others. All of this is necessary behavior for leaders who want to know what is happening in their organizations.

Leaders also need to standardize the way they do their work, enough to become more reliable to others. They need to support others, in success and in failure, and to effectively coach people as they learn to solve problems. Leaders who do this work, who learn to help others think through and make their own principle-based decisions, find they are not irreplaceable. Their leadership, however, is multiplied through influence.

In these chapters, you will hear from board members, executives, managers, and caregivers from all over the world who improved their organization's patient care by examining and changing their own behavior. Many of these leaders were good clinicians with great people skills who were promoted into management and picked up a few bad habits because they simply never stopped to consider how their style of solving problems fit with their organization's principles. Or, they are CFOs or human resources (HR) professionals who became true partners in the transformation because they learned to be vulnerable, to admit they did not know every answer.

This work also requires knowledge and use of a few practical tools, such as the Personal A3, a radar chart for tracking the user's improvement in their traits and behaviors, and an organizational x matrix for strategy. We provide depth into the use of these tools in section two of this book, before taking a longer view in the final chapter on the future of real healthcare transformations. What is a transformation, though? It is not clear when the definition of transformation became so limited. In 2019, it seemed to mean that a few processes were changed in one or more departments in order to create better efficiency. This is not the transformation we are talking about. We are talking about culture change that begins from within and radiates outward.

Instead of peppering you with fishbone diagrams and spaghetti charts in this book, we are inviting you to read the stories of others' work and examine your intentions, to deeply consider how other people feel after interacting with you, to question the type of outcomes you seek. This is how we begin to chart a more sustainable path to perfection.

PART I

Changes

What Change Looks Like

"I know I need to change. But how?"

The voice of the chief medical officer over the telephone was tight and unhappy. After 15 successful years as a medical specialist and another 3 years in leadership at this 500-bed American hospital, she was not used to stumbling on the job. She had gone to all the best schools and, in her experience, solutions were almost always within easy reach.

Now we were asking her to look at her hospital units in another way. Specifically, we were asking her to look without talking, without offering solutions. It was so much harder than she thought.

Like many doctors of her era and training, she was taught to take control of situations. If someone had a question, she liked to say, she had the answer. And because she always delivered that answer with a smile and a sense of camaraderie, people loved her.

Yet every day, this CMO left the hospital not knowing what she did not know. She knew there were problems of unknown origin and that she talked more than she listened. She wanted to change, she told Kim. The idea of learning from frontline medical staff about their problems made perfect sense. But how do you change decades of training?

AN OBSERVATION

So, a few weeks later, Kim arrived for a visit and went to gemba with the CMO to observe her in action. The CMO's first job in this personal coaching session was to observe a nurse going through the process of discharging a patient from the hospital. The CMO notified a nurse in advance that they would be observing the process in order to learn—not judge—and then listened as Kim listed the rules.

The CMO should ask no questions unless she saw something that was clearly putting the health and safety of a person at risk. If that happened, the gemba visit would be suspended while the situation was corrected. Otherwise, no questions. If the CMO could not help herself and absolutely had to speak, she was given a list of four acceptable questions that were focused on the purpose of the work. The CMO nodded; she was ready.

On the medical-surgical unit, a patient's lead nurse handled all the administrative and quality checks to be completed before a patient left the hospital, such as ensuring necessary testing had been performed, follow-up appointments had been scheduled, and prescription medications were dispensed.

In this case, the lead nurse was off shift and so the role fell to a nurse unfamiliar with the patient. The fact that he was being watched by the CMO and Kim probably made the nurse even more careful. He seemed determined to check every bit of information twice. But just as he confirmed that one test was done, a colleague alerted the nurse that he was getting a new patient. He left to complete that admission process, then returned and was interrupted again with questions about another case.

Still, this nurse diligently stepped through the discharge process, trying to get a patient safely home and free up a bed.

"Are you going to call the pharmacy and see if his prescriptions are ready?" the CMO asked.

The nurse nodded, interrupted his current task, placed that call, and continued on. Placing that call to the pharmacy was on the nurse's list; he just had not arrived there yet.

Back in the CMO's office, Kim asked how she thought the observation had gone.

"Why do you think the discharge process took so long?" the CMO asked in return. "We really need to streamline that process."

"Well, part of the problem may have been that the nurse was interrupted 13 times," Kim said. "And 5 of those times were by you."

MOTIVATION MATTERS

We begin with the story of this observation because moments like this are the raw material that culture is made of. We can make all the announcements that we like about transformation and organizational excellence, but none of it is real until leaders exhibit the behaviors that align with their words.

If a leader says she is there to observe and ends up directing the action, we know there is another agenda.

No matter how warm and personable this CMO was, every time she reminded the nurse to do a bit of work, she was saying that she knew the process better than he and that she was watching for compliance. And so they remained locked in their old roles: the know-it-all boss, the subservient underling.

This is a dynamic we have seen play out dozens of times, and it has led us to a simple lesson: motivations matter, and at gemba, people can see yours.

If nurses believe that a CMO wants to see the established process working well, they will work to make it go smoothly—glossing over the issues they struggle with every day.

If nurses believe that an executive is observing a process in order to see *what is* and find ways to help solve problems, they will be more comfortable pulling problems to the surface where everyone can examine them. Only then do we have the right environment for transformation.

The next question, of course, is, what will motivate that CMO to behave in a way that will help her see problems? To overcome those decades of training, she needed more than a few instructions on how to act. She—and every other executive and leader in that hospital—needed internal drivers. And for that, they needed common principles to guide them.

Creating a common code of fundamental truths that serve as the foundation for reasoning and action—in other words, principles—is what successful human organizations have always done. Whether people were banding together to learn or worship or create security, the organizations that lasted all had a common code to guide behavior. (Even if people did not always follow it perfectly.)

It turns out that the principles that will drive the right leadership behavior are pretty common. While every health system needs to collectively decide on its own principles, we will continue to cite the Shingo Institute principles (shown in Figure 1.1 on next page) throughout this book because they are the clearest example we know and perfectly align with the traits and behaviors required in organizational excellence:

- Create value for the patient.
- Create constancy of purpose.
- Think systemically.
- Assure quality at the source.
- Improve flow and pull.
- Seek perfection.
- Embrace scientific thinking.
- Focus on process (not people).
- Respect every individual.
- Lead with humility.

Let's return to that medical-surgical unit for a moment and see how the action—going to gemba to observe—would be different when driven by these principles. If our CMO thought of her task as being inseparable from principles such as respect for people and focus on process, it would have been difficult to interrupt the nurse as he worked through the discharge procedures. Instead of assuming the nurse would forget a step, the CMO would have been more curious about how well the process worked and whether the nurse had everything he needed. She definitely would have waited to ask questions until the patient's discharge was complete. That simple shift in focus creates an atmosphere where people are confident enough to point out problems.

FIGURE 1.1 **Shingo Principles**

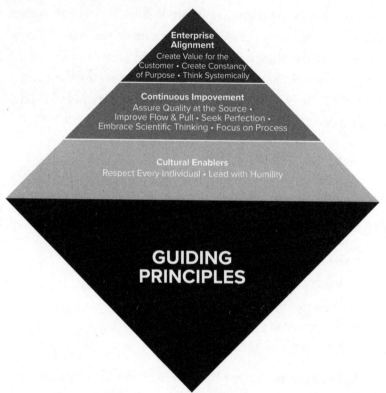

Throughout this book, we will be examining moments like this through the lens of different principles to get at the root of the behaviors that create a culture. At the same time, we will be looking at the actions people must take at every level of leadership to get to organizational excellence. Both types of change—internal (reflection on principles) and external (behaviors)—must occur at all levels of the organization.

Because there are so many moving parts to a transformation like this—with specific actions taking place at each level of leadership, tools being taught, and common principles being learned and adopted by all—it is easiest if we visualize how it all works from ground zero, the model cell.

THE STRATEGIC SIGNIFICANCE OF THE MODEL CELL

First, however, we need to define a model cell. In the past decade, the term has suffered a reduced reputation. In many organizations, what's called a model cell is actually just the experimental redesign of an area, separate from the rest of the organization and not of strategic importance. Improvement goals are often as low as 5 to 10 percent, and when it comes time to spread the work to other areas, it's just one pretty neat idea that is introduced around.

What this creates is an island of pretty good, surrounded by an organization that is unchanged. It is rarely worth the trouble.

A true model cell is the first act of a revolution. It strikes at the heart of an organization in that it begins with a business problem that is central to the organization's future. The model cell has an executive sponsor, not just the attention of an improvement team, and the goal is 50 to 100 percent improvement on the model cell's critical measures within six to nine months.

Does 50 to 100 percent improvement sound out of reach? In 2017, a 450-bed acute care medical center on the West Coast of the United States chose to focus on the ED to ensure that patients were seen faster and moved into the hospital more efficiently when required and that costs were controlled. Over the course of six months, workflows and job roles were redesigned, and a new management system was put in place. At the end of that six months, the number of people who gave up and left the

ED without treatment dropped by 98 percent, even while volume in the ED rose by 7 percent. The number of patients being boarded in the ER decreased by 29 percent, and the average cost for ED cases fell 13 percent.

The model cell is where the most tangible change begins. But that does not mean it is the first thing to happen in the organizational excellence transformation.

START AT THE BEGINNING

First, senior leadership needs to assess the organization's current conditions, its goals, and the gap between the two. As a group, they identify the few critical measures that become their True North (more on that in Chapter 4) and agree upon their principles. Only then does the leadership team have the necessary information to select the site for the model cell and choose the executive sponsor.

Now, the real learning begins. Leaders can choose one executive sponsor for the model cell, but all executives will need to lead various aspects of this transformation. The question is, what kind of people should lead the new world? What traits and behaviors are most desirable?

The leadership traits the team identifies should naturally flow from the principles being adopted. As a starting point, we advise groups to adopt these five fundamental leadership traits:

1. Willingness to change
2. Leading with humility
3. Curiosity
4. Perseverance
5. Self-discipline

These are not lofty goals. There are many studies that show leaders who display these traits are more effective at creating positive results.[1] More important, there are behaviors that can be learned and practiced to strengthen these traits. People are capable of change.

In order to change, of course, leaders must assess their current conditions and identify their goals and gaps. This means asking questions such as, "Am I glad to see a problem come to light? Do I really listen to my direct reports, or am I already thinking of a solution?" We highly recommend using a personal A3[2] for this work.

Once a team has identified their desired traits and assessed their own behavioral goals and gaps, we advise leaders to create a system of responsibility to one another. Maybe it will look like the mini 360-degree reviews created by UMass Memorial and detailed in Chapter 6, or the group reflections used by the California executive team profiled in Chapter 7. There are many ways to create responsibility, and all of them are legitimate as long as they provide respectful and timely feedback to leaders.

For most humans, there are gaps between how we think we are behaving and how others perceive us. Feedback and responsibility are our mirrors.

As leaders are learning new behaviors that support the work of the model cell, they will also be working with staff and medical personnel to redesign workflows in the target area and develop the routine of a daily management system.

---

1. Jim Collins, "Level 5 Leadership: The Triumph of Humility and Fierce Resolve," *Harvard Business Review*, July/August 2005.

2. The A3 is a more detailed version of the plan-do-study-act cycle. It is the scientific method for problem solving on a single sheet of A3-sized paper, expanded to include the business context and possible root causes for the problem. A personal A3 focuses on a leader's plan to practice desirable behaviors. Chapter 8 describes the personal A3 in much more detail and shows a sample.

Prior to the redesigned system being launched, executives and the improvement team will be preparing to spread the new way of designing workflow—not just the coolest idea from the model cell—to other areas. The management system will spread too. This means that senior leaders must become coaches, helping others to embrace principle-driven behaviors while solving their own problems.

This is the component of model cell work that most teams miss: behavior change. One thing will not happen without the other.

Over the years of doing this work, one of the most consistent truths we have seen is that new methods rarely take root without new leadership behavior, and so any benefit to the patient is fleeting. Yet new leadership behavior alone, of the kind we have outlined here, can create measurable improvements to patient outcome.

HOW LEADERSHIP BEHAVIOR CHANGES PATIENT OUTCOMES

In the fall of 2016, Dr. Susan P. Ehrlich, CEO of Zuckerberg San Francisco General Hospital (ZSFGH), did not set out to prove this point about leadership behavior. She just happened to have two major initiatives happening at the same time. One was her attempt to bring organizational excellence to the hospital, beginning with identifying True North and focusing on leadership behaviors. The second was the flu.

Flu season is pretty similar all over the country. It escalates in fall, peaks in late winter, and dissipates in late spring. And 2017 looked like it was going to be a bad year for flu. Still, Susan was determined to focus the 55 top leaders at ZSFGH on aligning their behaviors with the goals of organizational excellence.

They all began by defining their principles and five desirable leadership traits—willingness to change, humility, curiosity, perseverance, and self-discipline—and then worked with their peers in developing a personal A3[3].

Part of the leaders' personal A3 countermeasures plan was to create leadership standard work, including daily, weekly, and monthly activities that kept them on track toward achieving the organization's strategic goals, as well as their personal goals. They also used radar charts[4] and scheduled time for self-reflection so that they could gauge their personal growth toward the five desirable leadership traits.

The executives met in small groups to share their personal A3s with one another, and Susan convinced some of the leaders with more developed plans to go first. These peer-to-peer learning sessions proved to establish a camaraderie about the changes they were all going through. To create responsibility, they began with simple self-reflection but soon changed to 360-degree reviews, hoping to better see how others viewed their behavior.

This was no small task to take on during flu season. But the truth is, there is always an emergency or some budding crisis in a hospital. Perfect opportunities to take on extra work are rare.

This year, however, the flu kept getting worse. By late spring, patient volumes in the ED were not decreasing, but continuing to rise. In July 2016, the hospital's ED saw about 175 patients a day. In January 2017, the average patient population

---

3. See Chapter 8 for a complete description.
4. See Chapter 9 for details.

was 215 per day and rising. Volume did not peak until January 2018, at 240 patients per day.

In most hospitals, the reaction to this crisis would be the same: rising costs, patients turned away, and staff training sidelined while all hands responded to the emergency.

But Susan and her team doubled down on their plans. They established weekly standup rounds for leaders to review patient flow through the ED—which had just undergone a major overhaul as the hospital's model cell—and hospital inpatient services.

Leaders listened to frontline staff and one another as they focused on staffing, supplies, and patient transportation. They recruited colleagues to help them understand issues and spent time at the front line practicing their desired leadership traits, asking questions, and removing barriers.

In the thick of it, the leaders revisited their True North metrics and selected a few new performance metrics: percentage of time on ambulance diversion, mean ED length of stay, and number of patient days attributable to nonacute patients. Using A3s, they told each other the stories of multiple rapid experiments focused on areas where patient flow was getting stuck. They included staff ideas to address the problems and presented results to one another and to Susan, who made it a point to spend time at gemba with her team.

Patient volume in the ED remained high all summer, and as fall approached, and with it the promise of a new flu season, every executive at ZSFGH became engaged in this kind of problem solving. By the end of the year, 100 percent of leaders were trained in A3 thinking—an improvement of 23 percent. And 87 percent of leaders had adopted standard work for themselves—an improvement of 58 percent.

These behavioral changes had direct impact on quality scores that ZSFGH leaders were tracking and, by extension, on patient outcomes.[5] During 2017, while patient volume in the ED increased by 13 percent, important measures fell:

- Mean length of stay in the ED—decreased by 9 percent
- Time on ambulance diversion—decreased by 25 percent
- Days attributed to nonacute patients—decreased by 35 percent

This type of research linking leadership behavior to patient outcomes is still nascent. In fact, reliable scientific studies on the use of organizational excellence or continuous improvement tools—independent of leadership behaviors—is not robust, either. There were interesting studies at UC Berkeley in 2019, but to this point, healthcare leaders have not had the benefit of clear scientific conclusions regarding improvement methods.

What we do know is that organizations focused on continuous improvement provide better results for their patients. And leaders that consciously adopt principle-driven behaviors—and then coach others to do the same—ensure that continuous improvement work can thrive.

In this book, we focus on the behaviors required of leaders at all levels of a health system. Like most important initiatives, this change must begin at the top of an organization. But what we consider the top might be surprising to some.

---

5. These results were originally published in Susan P. Ehrlich, MD, MPP, and John S. Toussaint, MD, "Changing Leadership Behavior Gets Real Results," *NEJM Catalyst: Innovations in Care Delivery*, October 10, 2018.

Governing
the Change

The board of trustees is an underused and overlooked resource in just about every hospital and health system we know. Treated like distant, wealthy relatives holding the purse strings while far removed from daily realities, board members are fed a steady diet of carefully formatted reports at quarterly or monthly meetings and otherwise ignored. How often does a board of trustees know what is most vitally important to an organization?

Put this another way. If your CEO left tomorrow, would the board know the importance of having a humble leader? Or what a humble leader sounded like?

DROPPING THE BATON

There is so much to be done in a systemwide transformation—from mapping value streams and redesigning care processes to establishing a fully integrated daily management system—that perhaps it is understandable that those distant relations are forgotten. But we ignore them at our peril.

We know this because we are alumni of a cautionary tale. As the CEO (John) and president of hospitals (Kim) at ThedaCare, a large nonprofit cradle-to-grave health system in Wisconsin, we were proud of our national reputation. For more than a decade, ThedaCare was known as one of the best, most forward-thinking health systems in the United States.

John's first book, *On the Mend*, detailed the redesign of patient care and organizational culture we were undertaking at ThedaCare during the first decade of this century. After the book's release, we were bombarded with requests for tours and talks, which we gave to hundreds of visiting executive teams. And then Kim created a daily management system and wrote a book about it, *Beyond Heroes*. A lot more people came to see that. Alongside truly excellent organizations like Seattle Children's and the Cleveland Clinics, ThedaCare was known as a place to go see what good looked like.

As John was preparing to step down as CEO in 2008, he thought he understood succession planning in the context of ThedaCare's continuous improvement work. Or, at least, he was trying to.

John had polled his senior executive team for interest in the top job, selected the two best candidates, and created a two-year mentoring plan that aimed to emphasize or instill the qualities of a lean leader as he understood them: patience, curiosity, problem-solving skills, good communication, and a desire to be out in the middle of the action. He gave his top two candidates high-profile work assignments that reported results directly to the board and coached them on their presentations.

Focused as he was on presenting the board with the two very best candidates he could, John did not pay enough attention to the other side of the equation.

The board members were nearly unanimously fans of ThedaCare's results under John's leadership. But few understood exactly what was required to keep continuous improvement moving forward. Board members had been told about the concepts and strategy that we were using. But they had not been encouraged to adopt the thinking. So, how could they really know the most important characteristics of a lean leader?

The board selected one of the candidates John had mentored, and during the new CEO's tenure, ThedaCare was still an organization that was mostly running on the tenets of continuous improvement. Mostly. Erosion was visible in the organization's focus. There was less team-based problem solving. "Making the numbers" was sometimes more important than how the work got done.

The new CEO told people that a vision would emerge from the senior leadership team. The old vision—creating higher-quality, lower-cost care through lean thinking—was no longer his plan.

But the real deterioration was taking place far from the front line of care: new board members were selected without regard to their knowledge or appreciation of continuous improvement. And once elected to the board, they received no training in the ways of continuous improvement. They were told that ThedaCare had a stellar national reputation, but not how it got there.

So, when it was time to select a new CEO just a few years later, the ThedaCare board thought that continuous improvement was a concept from the organization's past, not its future. The new CEO brought his own initiatives, and most of the executives left for organizations that were following the principles of lean or organizational excellence.

THE BOARD AND CONTINUITY OF PURPOSE

Nearly every nonprofit hospital has the same board structure: populated by community leaders who volunteer their time and expertise in exchange for the honor of being chosen. (Some small percentage of health systems offer stipends for board members, but it rarely compensates for the time given.) Board members are chosen for their interest in serving and their abilities in areas such as finance, law, education, and medicine. The board usually has a single direct report—the CEO—and meets somewhere between four and a dozen times a year. One might think that the board manages the CEO, but it is often the other way around.

In the years since ThedaCare's initiative was dismantled, we have learned a lot about the board's role in creating a lasting culture of transformation. We have seen health systems in Canada, Oregon, and Massachusetts train their incoming board members, agree upon standard work for the board, and essentially create new partners in organizational excellence. Board engagement in continuous improvement is, it turns out, entirely possible as well as necessary.

And considering the fact that the average tenure for CEOs in US hospitals is about five years while board members serve about nine years,[1] we can make the argument that there can

---

1. "Hospital CEO Turnover Rate Remains Steady," American College of Healthcare Executives, June 14, 2018, press release.

be no continuity of purpose without instilling the principles and disciplines of continuous improvement in the board of trustees.

It is not just for CEO selection that we need trustees who understand the thinking of continuous improvement, of course. Boards create committees that have oversight responsibilities in finance, quality, and HR—all areas critical to organizational excellence. If the trustees who populate the finance, quality, and HR committees are going to understand the organization's true goals, they need to have at least some background in these concepts.

Trustees do not need to be lean practitioners. But they do need to understand what the organization is doing and why so that they can help keep strategy on track.

So, let's take a look at how a few forward-thinking organizations have addressed selection, orientation, and training of new board members.

ST. CHARLES HEALTH SYSTEM: A BETTER WORKING BOARD

"I think we were like most boards. When we needed new board members, we would look around the room and say, *OK, we need another lawyer or someone with experience in mergers. Who can we get?* Our selection process was all networking," says Daniel F. Schuette, board chair of St. Charles Health System in Oregon.

A four-hospital system and the largest employer in central Oregon, St. Charles's board structure was fairly typical, with 11 to 15 members at any one time, each of whom served three-year terms with no term limit. Some people were naturally more outspoken; others were reluctant to share their opinions. If there was a doctor on the board—and there was usually just one—that member could have outsized influence.

In short, the St. Charles board was similar to most governing bodies in healthcare. And then they hired a new CEO in 2014 who said he needed a mechanism to solve problems and wanted to introduce lean thinking to St. Charles. Right away, Dan Schuette was worried.

The new CEO was impressive and obviously capable, but Dan thought, "Uh-oh. Here we go chasing some shiny ball."

A longtime financial advisor, Dan said he had seen organizations go down such roads before, adopting new management or quality systems and all the jargon that went with them, and it always seemed like more noise than revolution. There had been a lean initiative at St. Charles years earlier that never quite got traction. After that it was Triple Aim[2], then Quadruple Aim,[3] and then initiative exhaustion set in. A caregiver survey showed that distrust and change fatigue were higher in the practitioner ranks than anyone wanted.

On another board Dan served on, he found a guy whose résumé said he had a black belt in lean, so Dan asked him about it. What did he think about this lean stuff? The guy said, "Oh, we don't do that anymore," and Dan grew more worried still.

Along with another board member, Dan approached the new lean consultant St. Charles was using and asked him what the board—or the board chair—could do to help out with this lean stuff. The consultant said he didn't know; nobody had ever asked him that before.

---

2. An approach to healthcare improvement, defined by the Institute for Healthcare Improvement, that has organizations give equal weight to improving the patient experience, improving the health of populations, and reducing per-capita costs.

3. Essentially the same as IHI's Triple Aim but includes an element of employee/provider satisfaction.

Incoming CEO Joe Sluka, on the other hand, had very clear ideas. He wanted the board not just to adopt lean thinking but to help drive the change. He talked to them about the importance of the Shingo principles and suggested they consider having a rapid improvement event of their own.

"Of course, we weren't going to try and improve a process in the hospitals because the board has no business getting involved in operations. Our job is to help set vision and strategy for the future. We consider things like how the organization needs to respond to changes in payment systems, for instance," Dan says. "I'm not sure how we might use lean thinking to address those issues in the future, but we thought it could help us with some immediate needs."

For instance, board members agreed, they really needed to improve the way they found and appointed new board members. And it would be nice if the bimonthly agenda were a little more focused. Did they all really need to read 400 pages of material before every meeting?

So, with an eye toward addressing problems at the board level, the group agreed to a three-day board retreat led by the new CEO—with help from a consultant and an HR executive—to learn the concepts and tools and put them to use.

"We talked a lot about the board's role in a lean journey and then about how to apply the thinking to some of our own processes," says Megan Haase, a board member, family nurse practitioner, and the CEO of Mosaic Medical, which operates federally qualified health centers throughout central Oregon, providing healthcare to underserved populations and the general community. "We learned how to use standard work to create agendas that would get us talking about what is really important. We were able to eliminate what was non-value-added and that helped to cut down our 400-page premeeting packets to something like 50 pages."

Those smaller, more focused premeeting packets were a minor revelation. Even more revelatory were their talks on how leaders should behave in this environment.

Thinking about the Shingo principles and the leadership traits that flow from those—willingness to change, leading with humility, curiosity, perseverance, and self-discipline—the board members realized that they needed to recruit new trustees for traits and behaviors, not just for skills.

Joe Sluka had already been working with HR at St. Charles to adopt behavior-based interviewing at the executive level to ensure he could populate his leadership team with people who were inclined toward continuous improvement, even if they did not know it yet. Joe shared with the board some of the interview questions they had developed. With some editing and rethinking, the board adopted behavior-based questions for their next interviews.

"The interview process has become more intense, more emotional, both for the person being interviewed and for us," Megan says. "Our questions now are along the lines of, 'Tell me about a time that you lost trust with a team and then worked to regain it.'

"But now, it becomes very clear quite quickly which candidates will lead in a way that aligns with the lean model. I've been so impressed with it that we've begun using it at Mosaic," Megan added.

Now, if the board needs another lawyer or a clinician or a business specialist, they know they need to widen their pool of potential candidates. Just knowing a guy personally is no longer enough. They need enough candidates to be selective.

In-depth questions with new trustees have had real bene-fits for the board meetings, too. Potential board members have a much better idea of the kind of work being done on St. Charles's board and the seriousness with which the other trustees regard the position. In short, they are better prepared.

And in the four years since St. Charles's board began using behavior-based interviewing techniques, the atmosphere in the board meetings has been tangibly improved. Where there used to be cliques, silent resentment, and the occasional bomb thrower, there are now people with a common idea of what a productive board meeting looks like.

"There's more listening now, and we really work at humble inquiry," Dan says. "We recognize bullying behavior and call it out."

Trustees also have mentoring relationships, in which each new board member is paired with an existing one to assist in understanding the work and how it is done.

Existing board members—those who began serving before anyone thought of hiring for behaviors—have used radar charts and personal A3s to help them enhance or adopt desirable lead-ership behaviors.

At this point, there will be plenty of board members and CEOs reading this who will be asking, *Is this really necessary?* Do people really need to look deep within their personal beliefs and alter their leadership styles in order to serve on a commu-nity hospital board?

The answer is *yes*, if they want to be useful and engaged in the future.

For most of the twentieth century, there was one standard business model for healthcare in the United States and many other countries: get people into the hospital and get paid. Heads in beds. Now the model is turning away from fee-for-service and toward population health, in which health systems make money by offering integrated care and keeping people out of expensive hospitals. That means every hospital CEO needs strong strategic partners to help create a workable plan to be ready for that future.

Should your health system be creating extensive care-at-home initiatives for the elderly and chronically ill? Do you need different facilities, a different mix of skill sets? *What should a hospital look like when you are trying to keep people out of it?* These are the questions a board must consider. And that means trustees are going to need excellent processes that help them decide strategic direction, including a standard problem-solving process.

As representatives of the community, board members are also responsible for making sure that the executive team's True North and strategic vision aligns with community needs. This is a critical function as health systems begin redefining their roles. Does the community need a world-class research facility, smaller surgical and urgent care centers, or is it an aging, shrinking population that requires new ideas in affordable long-term care?

The board needs to be able to work together effectively to help explore and answer these questions. And, in many ways, that is a whole new role.

ST. MARY'S GENERAL HOSPITAL: MAKING AN INVESTMENT IN THE BOARD

"Boards have changed a lot in the last decade, especially as changes in healthcare have multiplied," says Christine

Henhoeffer, RN and a past board chair of St. Mary's General Hospital, a 150-bed acute care hospital and regional cardiac center in Kitchener, Ontario. "It used to be that you received a package, read it, and listened to the presentation. We didn't ask challenging questions. It wasn't expected. Meetings were pleasant. You did your duty and hoped to get out of there early."

But somewhere around 2010, St. Mary's started having financial trouble and meetings became longer and filled with more pressing questions. People thought the hard patch would be over soon, but it was really just the first signal that bigger changes would be coming.

CEO Don Shilton, a champion of lean, was trying to bring transformation to the ED first and having some typical islands-of-excellence issues. St. Mary's was usually rated in the middle of the pack, quality-wise, among Canadian hospitals, and he was sure it could do better. So he came to the board with a plan to spread lean thinking throughout the organization by having 1,000 frontline improvements implemented in the next year. It was a big goal for a stressed organization, Christine thought.

But she read the book that Don gave them all—*On the Mend*—and was intrigued. With three other board members, Christine made the trek to Wisconsin to visit ThedaCare and attend an introductory course in lean thinking.

The response she got when she was introduced to other healthcare leaders attending the sessions was curious. "What are you doing here?" they asked. Christine laughs at the memory.

"They could not understand why board members would be interested in this lean stuff," Christine says. "Still, we went to gemba and huddles on the units and we could see this really was a way to make things better for our patients. We went there not knowing our key performance indicators or what St. Mary's targets were. But we left knowing that we needed to find out."

Over the next two years, Don continued to champion lean thinking and Christine, in 2013, became board chair. With help from Don, Christine began a focused education initiative at board meetings. She convinced the other trustees to commit to attending a huddle in a hospital unit, and to visit ThedaCare sometime in the next two years. Together, board members read articles on lean thinking in healthcare and held generative discussions, with a different board member leading the discussion each month.

"Sure, there was some pushback. People started saying we had drunk the Wisconsin Kool-Aid," Christine says. "There would be knots of people talking in the parking lot later. I got emails concerned about the longer meeting times. But when people went to a huddle or went to ThedaCare, they got it. They came back enthused."

"They saw engaged staff who were solving problems," recalls Don Shilton, who retired as CEO in 2018. "That was exciting. So, we started bringing staff into the meetings to present a problem they had solved. It became more real."

In the hospital, however, the early energy of transformation had begun to fade. Only 10 out of 40 original huddles were still active. Don asked the board for help with a reset. He believed they needed to create a full daily management system, and his aspirations came with a big price tag—somewhere close to $1 million.

Board members were cautious. Were huddles all that important? What would this daily management system do?

Don suggested the board try a huddle of their own. Just 15 minutes, standing up, at the start of each meeting, he said. Half of the huddle was a performance review, looking over the hospital's most important metrics. Each metric was aligned under its related True North category and labeled with a red dot if the work was not meeting goals, or a green dot if it was. They only talked about the metrics that were in the red, to ask what was being done to correct course.

The second half of the huddle—which was added to their routine several months later—was problem solving to improve board governance. For instance, the meetings often went too long. They looked at the sheer number of agenda items they had every month that were pro forma. Each required a reading and a vote, even though there was never any discussion. Someone had the idea of creating a consent category: all agenda items that needed approval but not discussion were presented as a single item. That shaved about 15 valuable minutes off the general meeting, leaving more time and less grumbling for the huddle or those article reviews.

After about a year of huddles, though, some board members were running out of improvement ideas. Maybe they did not need to have huddles anymore, they told Don. Maybe they were as improved as they could be.

"I'll admit, I was alarmed when some of them said they did not see the value in huddles anymore," Don says. "The fact that the board had a regular huddle carried a lot of weight in the organization. They were a positive example for everyone."

Don asked the trustees to reconsider. They agreed to talk about it, at least, and to use an A3 to guide them as they discussed the relative merits of each element of the huddle. It turned out parts of the huddle were unanimously valued, so they came up with a structure that everyone could agree upon.

It was a valuable lesson in the importance of revisiting standard work on a regular basis to consider how it could be improved. More important still, the board was reminded of its importance to the rest of the organization. Trustees have a part in setting the tone of an organization. They signal to others what is important every time they set foot in the hospital. Attending huddles, visiting units, and asking respectful questions is a far different message than making a beeline to the boardroom and only staying for their private meetings.

"And when trustees go to the ED and see a busy place dealing with a lot of mental health issues, or the consequences of working in an old building with narrow doorways and equipment in the hallways, that's a lot different than hearing about it in the boardroom," Don says.

By 2016, the results of organizational excellence at St. Mary's were helping Don to make his case. In the three years since the organization had recommitted to lean, frontline improvements had helped cut the number of patient falls in half. Hospital-acquired infections were reduced by 60 percent, and the cost per inpatient hospital stay was reduced to 20 percent less than the Canadian average. The people of St. Mary's were most proud of having the lowest Hospital Standardized Mortality Ratio (HSMR)[4] in Canada twice in five years.

Christine and Don are united in their advice to other boards that need to begin learning about continuous improvement. First, they say, go see: have everyone attend a huddle and take groups to see excellent hospitals. Then, encourage board members to get involved by using the tools to solve some of their own problems. Meetings too long? Need new trustees that can think systemically and show constancy of purpose? Create an A3 and agree upon the problem and the current condition before considering countermeasures.

---

4. The HSMR is the observed number of deaths divided by the expected number of deaths in a given hospital for a given year; it is expressed as a percentage.

SUCCESSION PLANNING NEVER STOPS

Of course, the most important issue a board considers is selecting a new CEO. Continuity of the leadership required in this environment—humble, curious, disciplined, and committed to improvement—is the reason we actively encourage boards to learn about and use continuous improvement. The question is, does it work?

As of this writing, there has been just one CEO turnover in an organization using continuous improvement at the board level. When Don Shilton announced that he was leaving St. Mary's in 2018, we watched closely to see what the board would do.

We were encouraged by the board's selection of a physician leader from Ottawa who was an enthusiastic advocate of continuous improvement. Nobody could foresee, however, that within a week of Dr. Andrew Falconer's arrival at St. Mary's as president, the CEO at his former hospital would die. Five months later, Dr. Falconer accepted the invitation to return to his former organization as CEO, regretfully leaving St. Mary's board with a new decision and a realization.

"We really need to do more work on succession planning, on being prepared for any eventuality," says Scott Smith, current St. Mary's board chair and president of High Performance Solutions and Consortiums in Ontario, which operates several co-learning networks focused on organizational excellence. "This situation proved our gap.

"Now we're looking for someone with experience in a lean organization and, if we can't find that, for someone with the leadership competencies and characteristics that will help us grow our current system. Someone who understands A3 thinking, is people focused, and leads with humility."

That is the list of characteristics that should guide any board of trustees looking for a new CEO. But will the trustees know that?

UMASS MEMORIAL: BEHAVIORAL EXPECTATIONS

About 560 miles south and east of St. Mary's, at UMass Memorial Health Care in Worcester, MA, CEO Eric Dickson, MD, talks about succession planning in every board meeting. They talk about what would happen if he—or anyone else in a critical role—were to get hit by a beer truck. Eric asks every senior leader to put a possible successor in place whenever they take vacation or have even a few days leave. The next step, he says, is to write a succession plan into the board's standardized work.

That's right. The board of trustees at UMass is guided by standard work, and it is the first instance we have seen of the discipline at the board level.

For their four formal meetings per year, plus monthly strategy sessions, the 17-member board follows a standard work template as they talk through strategy and metrics. (Leadership each year chooses the 10 most important metrics, including key performance and key behavioral indicators, on which to focus.) There is standard work to guide them as they develop new strategic plans and standard work to execute those plans.

In fact, Eric does not really use the term *organizational excellence* or *lean* to describe what they do at UMass. "It's really just standardized work processes and a standardized management system," he says. "It's got to be standardized before it can be improved."

Eric hired an executive coach with experience and expertise in the Toyota Production System and, from his work with her, created four simple principles to guide their work:

- Have a standardized process that can be continuously improved.
- Make waste visual for all to see.
- Respect everyone.
- Engage everyone in improvement every day.

Eric strongly believes that a system like this requires that everyone is engaged—including the board—and that means everyone at UMass needs to believe in the future of it.

"If I get hit by that beer truck, I want them to be ready," Eric says. "Look across the country at these great programs in health systems that ended because they were dependent on one strong leader. That's why I have board members attend a continuous improvement training session, management training, and at least one huddle."

The training in continuous improvement for board members at UMass includes learning the expected behaviors, which are the same for everyone and are displayed on walls throughout the hospitals and the boardroom as the standards of respect. They are: listen, be kind, acknowledge, be a team player, communicate, and be responsive.

Every leader and manager receives an annual review that includes what Eric describes as a mini-360, in which the reviewer checks in with the person's peers, direct reports, and bosses on the question of respectful behavior. Board members undergo the review, too.

All of this was especially necessary because when Eric returned to UMass in 2013 as CEO, there was a good bit of shouting and disrespect at the board meetings. To be fair, everyone was under stress. There had been four years of declining operating performance. Nurses voted in favor of going out on a 24-hour strike two months after Eric arrived. Hospitals were shut down and replacement nurses brought in at a cost of $10 million.

Three months after that, the controller realized his office had been miscalculating debt service coverage and default was likely. UMass Memorial Health Care bonds were downgraded to "junk" status. Eric had to oversee the layoffs of 600 people while seven buildings were sold. A psychiatric patient murdered another patient on the ward. And 50 percent of the organization's executives turned over in the first 16 months of his tenure.

The board of trustees, meanwhile, did not have experience with creating an environment of respect. And it showed. Five board members are appointed by the state; the rest had been selected by the former CEO, whose departure had not been planned or pleasant.

Fortunately, there was one board member who, shortly after Eric's arrival as CEO, stuck up her hand with a proposal. She had received leadership training from the organizational guru W. Edwards Deming, she said, and she thought what they really needed to decide first was the behaviors they wanted to exhibit.

The idea resonated with a number of trustees who were tired of the acrimony, so they made a short list of behaviors and read them out at the beginning of every meeting. Because they had all agreed to the behaviors, it was not considered confrontational to offer gentle reminders to people who slipped.

After a few months, they did not need to read out the expected behaviors at the beginning of every meeting anymore, so they had the behaviors printed on a sign and displayed. Within a couple of years, the sign was moved to some back closet because nobody needed to refer to it anymore. Their expectations about how meetings should proceed had become governed by standardized work instead of egos. Respect was part of the culture.

Some of the change in the boardroom environment has surely been more organic than planned and voted upon. A lot of it has to do with Eric's style, his belief systems. Under prior leadership, there was a heavy top-down management style. The CEO had been firmly in charge and ran the meetings—like so many CEOs do—like a zero-sum game.

This is not an unusual attitude in US companies. Boards are often seen as necessary evils, a monthly exercise in herding cats that the CEO does artfully or not. Rarely does the top executive really use the board's various talents to full effect.

But Eric's favorite sentence is, "I don't know." He will say that he does not know enough about marketing or digital therapeutics or finance structures and ask board members if they have expertise or they can find someone who does who can coach him through the finer points. When he gets help like this, he says, he can be more fully engaged in conversations with his on-staff experts. With multiple points of view, he gets a richer dialogue. And board members are reminded of their value.

"Board members are here volunteering because they actually want to serve. They don't want to just be managed by a CEO," Eric says. "I serve on seven other boards, and I can tell you when there is tension in board meetings it is because the CEO doesn't really want to hear from the board. People know when they are not valued."

Things at UMass Memorial improved over the first six years of Eric's tenure. Some 70,000 frontline staff improvement ideas had been implemented as of spring 2019, and every year now, there is a Champions of Excellence celebration that includes $10,000 in innovation awards.

Improvements have helped drop inpatient mortality at Marlborough Hospital by 43 percent and at UMass Memorial Medical Center by 21 percent between 2016 and 2019.

There are still problems. One year, the health system had tens of millions in surplus funds. The following year, when managed care health plans stepped up to care for a lot of Medicaid patients, patient demand fell, and UMass was back in the red. While 72 percent of people would "definitely" recommend the UMass Medical Center, the goal for that metric is 83 percent. It is improved, but the gap remains clear.

So, Eric would be the first one to tell you he still needs the expertise and problem solving of an active board. We all do.

In this emerging work we have been doing with boards, we have seen some practices—such as those stand-up huddles that start out every meeting at St. Mary's—have great impact. We do not recommend, however, that an organization jumps into huddles and rules of behavior with trustees until everyone agrees upon the direction they are heading.

For health systems beginning the work of engaging the board, the first step must be some introduction to lean ideas. This includes having trustees go to see continuous improvement at work in the hospital and inviting the people responsible for frontline improvement to present their work to the board.

Any introduction will also naturally include a discussion of the organization's principles and the leadership behaviors that must spring from those. Shingo principles such as *create value for the patient, create constancy of purpose*, and *think systemically* are particularly relevant for a board of trustees. This is, after all, what we value in board members—the ability to consider the health of the entire organization, to think in the long term, and to remember that they advocate for and serve the community.

Along with principles and behaviors, the board should also become familiar with True North. In fact, a good board should become keepers of the True North—ensuring that these core goals reflect the community's needs, that the organization is always aimed toward meeting those needs, and that only the critical few initiatives are given time. A good board should be able to assist the CEO in deselection or, at the very least, track the number of initiatives and weigh them against the organization's strategy and resources.

As a learning exercise, each of these boards used A3 thinking and other tools to solve some of their own problems, such as overly long meetings and premeeting reports.

We also recommend that boards begin to measure what matters—for example:

- The length of board meetings, in minutes
- The number of pages in the premeeting packet
- The number of minutes spent on strategy discussions, per meeting
- Is succession planning discussed?
- How deep in the organization is succession planning practiced?

Figure 2.1 (see next page) shows a sample board assessment, which is valuable for any organization that wants to determine what good looks like at the board level.

When the board begins looking for new members, what does that process look like? At St. Charles and UMass Memorial, there is standardized work in place for both recruitment and interviews. St. Charles's focus is on behaviors, UMass emphasizes skills and experience when looking for new members. (Eric was determined to bring a millennial on board, for instance, to gain the youth perspective.)

FIGURE 2.1 **Board Assessment Questionnaire**

This questionnaire can be used to rate an organization's progress in using improvement processes. Rate statements 1 through 17 on a scale of 1–4 as follows:

1. **Not started.** No continuous improvement program.

2. **Beginning.** Planning has begun, activities may have started, but no significant engagement and no significant progress.

3. **Growing.** Teaching, engaging, succeeding, struggling, and failing are all occurring as the teams make slow, steady, and sometimes painful progress forward. Leaders, physicians, and associates alike are becoming progressively more involved, more committed, and more capable of learning from both successes and failures.

4. **Sustaining.** The organization's principle-driven lean behaviors can be described as teaching, mentoring, supporting, encouraging, enabling, humbling, steady, predictable, teachable, engaged, committed, and disciplined. Cultural behaviors drive many successes and also occasional failures with A3 thinking (or an equivalent structured problem-solving method) being applied in all cases.

1. Board members have been trained and participated in three gemba visits per year and have practiced asking open-ended questions. Board members have participated in at least one education session on improvement thinking this year.

2. Board members are offered opportunities to tour best practice improvement organizations. Some members participate every year.

3. The board has clearly defined in writing and practice the role of governance versus management.

4. The board evaluates improvement plans and organizational performance at each board meeting with a set of clear top-level metrics (True North) for quality, safety, cost, patient satisfaction, and staff engagement.

5. The board works with management on a regular basis (at least three times a year) to define and reevaluate the strategic direction of the organization.

6. The board understands and reviews management's A3 presentations at each board meeting.

7. The board exhibits ideal behaviors in the practice of governance as outlined in a written board code of conduct.

8. The board has defined the behavioral expectations for Board members.

9. The board has at least one member that has extensive experience with lean/improvement.

10. The board has a system to assure board member succession planning includes questions regarding potential members' willingness to learn the lean method and practice it at the governance level.

11. There is a process to onboard new members to the organization's improvement methodology.

12. The board has developed an internal CEO succession plan that includes identifying potential successors, regular updates on their progress and experiences, and a focus on the behavioral traits that would allow the person to be an effective lean CEO.

13. At a minimum of once a year, the board reviews the organization's commitment to lean methods, outcomes of lean management, and leader development across administrative and medical staff.

14. Board members regularly identify areas for improvement in governance practices.

15. At least one committee is practicing some aspect of lean thinking in their governance activities including but not limited to improvement projects identified by board members using PDSA (plan-do-study-act) thinking for problem solving or Pareto analysis of board problems.

16. Some portion of every board meeting is devoted to improving the board's practices.

17. Board performance and improvements are visual, displayed where all can see them.

All three of the health systems introduced here have placed careful attention on introducing new board members into their ecosystem. They all offer some kind of organizational excellence training, and then the CEO and board veterans talk to new members one-on-one about behavioral expectations and the principles that guide the organization.

This is all-important work because the board can be thought of as the constancy of a health system. A majority of the trustees will very likely outlast a CEO and choose the next. Without them on the side of continuous improvement, the memory of it will be lost. And the CEOs you will meet in the next chapter will likely be aberrations instead of what we all really need, which is the coming wave.

Change and the Chief Executive

When Kathy Krusie began her rise through the ranks of hospital leadership in Cedar Rapids, Iowa, she worried a little about her personality. With every promotion, she was told that her teams and superiors valued her. But when she looked across the national landscape of executive leadership, she wondered how she would fit in.

Jack Welch, former CEO of General Electric, was writing straight from the gut about making bold, controversial moves. Business publications lionized the dealmakers, the iconoclasts, the lone-wolf genius.

"That was what success looked like. But that wasn't how I was wired," Kathy says. "I'm from the Midwest and a bit of an introvert. I never felt like I had all the answers. If rushing up on stage to tell my story was the way to be a leader, I didn't see how I could."

As her organization, Mercy Medical Center, began a journey into continuous improvement, however, Kathy saw the possibility of a shift in the definition of leadership. Teaching people to solve problems with an A3, coaching teams to use the tools and be curious, cheering on good work instead of taking credit—that felt like leadership to her.

As a senior vice president and leader of Mercy's continuous improvement effort, Kathy emphasized respect and humility and saw how the tenor of the hospital changed as a result. But maybe, she thought, Mercy was an anomaly.

In 2010 she was offered a job as CEO of St. Joseph's Regional Health Center in Bryan, Texas, and the question returned stronger than ever: What kind of leader should she be? St. Joseph's was a health system dedicated to continuous improvement, but would Texans appreciate her humility?

Fortunately, a new model of leadership was emerging around that time following the research and writing of Jim Collins. In his 2001 book, *Good to Great*, and a later *Harvard Business Review* article on what he called Level 5 leadership,[1] Collins detailed the results of a five-year study of hundreds of US businesses showing that companies who made the transition from good to great were led by focused, humble leaders, not big personalities.

"The ideas resonated, especially because he had some solid research showing this kind of leadership was getting results," Kathy says. "Humility is easy for me. There is also a time and place for leaders to set the vision, construct guardrails, and get

---

1. Jim Collins, "Level 5 Leadership: The Triumph of Humility and Fierce Resolve," *Harvard Business Review*, July/August 2005.

people moving in the right direction, of course. Jim Collins showed the success of a leadership model with both traits."

Still thinking about balancing her personality with her career goals, Kathy arrived in Texas aware that people would view her through the lens of other CEOs they had known. Chief executives mostly cared about money, people thought. That's because money was what CEOs mostly talked about.

"I wanted to counteract that. I wanted to show that I believe healthcare is personal," Kathy says. "Then again, as an introverted person, I'm not used to showing people how I really feel. Maybe my reticence comes off as stone-faced, sometimes.

"I decided that I really needed to show people I cared, but in a way that was authentic for me. If it wasn't true, people would know. So, I made it a priority to do informal gemba walks. Whenever I left my office to go to a meeting or anything, I would plot a course through a unit or work area and chat with people there."

As all introverts know, chatting with strangers is not the easiest activity. If Kathy was just idly saying hello, she might have stopped walking into new places after a week or two. But St. Joseph's was committed to visual management in most areas. Kathy found that conversations were easiest if she looked at the visual management board in the department first. Then she could turn to a person in the area, introduce herself, and compliment some bit of work or ask about a current issue. The point was not to put a person on the spot, but to get to know that person a little better.

Soon, the new CEO was walking around St. Joseph's, greeting people she knew, hearing about what was happening on units far from her office.

In Jim Collins's article on Level 5 leadership, he recounts a conversation he had with a group of top executives. A woman in the group, who said that she rose to CEO in part because of her strong ego, asked if this kind of humble, focused leadership could be taught. Could she learn to change? Collins said he did not know.

But we think that Kathy's story, like the stories of other CEOs you will read in this chapter, proves that this kind of leadership can be learned by anyone who is willing. And the principles and behaviors of continuous improvement are what you can use to get there.

Maybe it seems like Kathy, a self-effacing Midwesterner, was already more than halfway there to leading with humility. In that regard, she had an advantage. But there are other equally important principle-driven behaviors for a CEO to live, and those, she had to work for.

Before we get into those behaviors, though, let's step up a level to principles.

For each level of leadership, we can highlight a few principles that are critical to the role. While executives and organizations all have their own unique challenges, it is useful to also consider the universal truths.

We believe that the most important Shingo-identified principles for a CEO to embrace are creating value for the patient, constancy of purpose, and systemic thinking. The observable behaviors or traits that tell us whether a CEO is living those principles are leading with humility, which Kathy has nailed, and self-discipline, which almost every CEO needs to work on.

Self-discipline is most easily observed in CEOs who follow and display standard work, have regularly scheduled visits to gemba, and take time for reflection at least weekly. Here is the good news: these are also the three practices—standard work, gemba walks, personal reflection—that we have seen CEOs use most successfully to improve as leaders.

TWO HOSPITALS IN SOUTH AFRICA: THE CEO BUDDY SYSTEM

For instance, if you ever had the opportunity to meet Grey Dube, CEO of Leratong Regional Hospital outside of Johannesburg, South Africa, you would probably agree that he seems to come by respectfulness quite naturally. Soft-spoken and courtly, he is known by all as Mr. Dube.[2]

As any leader can tell you, however, our own best attributes are not necessarily reflected in our organizations, and when his 855-bed regional hospital began its lean journey in 2015, respect and humility were not cultural priorities. Patients had long waits for treatment; medical files were routinely lost. Physicians tended to show up late to their clinics, often beginning their days at 11 a.m. instead of when the clinic opened at 8 a.m.

In 2015, Mr. Dube had been chief executive for 10 years and had learned to trust his instincts and intuition to make good decisions. He had plenty of practice at this since he spent most of his time fighting fires. Every day, people came to him with immediate problems to be solved and he did that. But he had begun to think there had to be a better way. So, he and his staff began training with Lean Institute Africa, learning to use scientific thinking in teams to address the processes they used to deliver healthcare.[3]

A lot of people were energized to do better work. But people were still doing things mostly in their own way. They had a hard time embracing a common working system.

---

2. We use first names for everyone in this book because we strive for equality and encourage everyone to see past people's titles and degrees. Since we have never heard Mr. Dube called by anything but his title and last name, however, we will use it here.

3. Lean Institute Africa is a member of the Lean Global Network, founded by Jim Womack and Dan Jones.

"We could achieve improvements, but we could not sustain them," Mr. Dube said.

On the advice of their Lean Institute Africa advisor, and with the support of Gauteng Department of Health, which oversees all hospitals and medical services in the province,[4] Mr. Dube went to Wisconsin in 2017 to look at a daily management system and learn what such methods needed from a leader.

With Mr. Dube on that trip was his friend and colleague Gladys Bogoshi, CEO of Charlotte Maxeke Johannesburg Academic Hospital, also in Gauteng province. A teaching hospital with 1,068 beds and 5,700 people on staff, including 700 physicians and 2,500 nurses, Charlotte Maxeke had problems that were very much like Mr. Dube's: getting all those people working together, unified by the same motivations, to improve care for their patients.

There was much opportunity for improvement. In the neonatal unit, for instance, preventable mortality was 20.5 per 1,000 patients in 2017; the hospital-acquired infection rate on the unit ranged from 7 percent to 11.5 percent that year, and they recorded an average of 14 different bacteria strains.[5]

"It used to be that porters—staff members in the supply chain—did not see themselves as being involved in patient care," Gladys says. "But even the finance people are healthcare workers."

One of the earliest model cells, in fact, was set up to address just this problem. In the Gauteng health system, some people with kidney failure receive dialysis treatment at home instead of going to a clinic. The hospitals were responsible for

---

4. Gauteng is the smallest of South Africa's nine provinces, but it is also the most densely populated. Johannesburg is the capital.

5. For comparison, the total infant mortality rate in the United States was 5.8 per 1,000 live births in 2017; in South Africa, infant mortality was 27.5 per 1,000 live births that same year.

getting supplies to the patients' homes on a timely, regular cadence. Too frequently, patients were thrown into crisis simply because they did not have adequate supplies due to late or non-delivery.

"We gathered people from finance, supply-chain clerks, and nurses into the same room to discuss this. Finance people said the fault was in the supply chain, and supply-chain clerks said no, it was the other way around. Nurses were in the middle," Gladys says.

"So, we asked a nurse to explain exactly what happened to a person who did not receive their treatment on time. A nurse got up and described how it felt to have fluid gathering in your lungs, putting pressure on the heart, how a person could then only take small, shallow breaths and would start to turn blue as their whole body swelled."

That is what happened to people—who could be neighbors and family members—when paperwork was unfinished. It did not matter whose fault it was. Only the patient suffered. Someone said out loud, "Oh! We're killing the patients."

Together, the groups began investigating where their processes broke down. They were learning, Gladys says, what it meant to step out of their silos and think first about the patients.

At the same time, she and Mr. Dube were learning what it meant to be disciplined and humble. Through a 10-month series of telephone coaching sessions, we talked with them about True North, strategic initiatives, principles, and the leadership behaviors that were necessary to energize change.

Some things—such as organizational principles and key performance measures—were chosen for them, by the Gauteng Department of Health. But Gladys and Mr. Dube enthusiastically embraced the idea of choosing the behaviors they wanted to display and tracking progress toward their goals.

"We began by writing down everything we did, every day," Mr. Dube says. "We learned to look at our activities through the lens of what benefited the patient. We learned to ask, 'Why should I spend time on this if it doesn't affect the patients?'"

Like Susan Ehrlich in San Francisco, they also used radar charts (Figure 3.1; shown and described in detail in Chapter 9) and regular reflection periods to map their strengths and weaknesses in the five traits: willingness to change, leading with humility, curiosity, perseverance, and self-discipline. In each area, they chose behaviors that were emblematic of the trait they wanted and rated themselves from one to five.

FIGURE 3.1   **One of Mr. Dube's Earliest Radar Charts That Helped Guide His Behavioral Change**

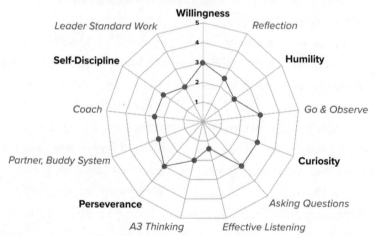

Under willingness to change, for instance, both Gladys and Mr. Dube typically scored high. (Gladys cannot remember scoring below a four.) Like many CEOs, they were action-oriented and ready to take on whatever challenges came their way.

But the activities that indicate a leader's willingness to change include keeping regular reflection periods and creating (and displaying) standard work. Leaders who think "Change is easy for me" might have to reassess that statement based on how they really spend their time. After all, if a leader has no standard work, how can she expect to assess and improve how she spends her time? And if a leader does not take time to reflect on his behavior, how can he change?

"For me, I really needed that reflection," Mr. Dube says. "An hour before I go home, I ask myself what I did that contributed to the morale of my staff and what I did that irritated my staff. What could I do better? I do this three times a week, and it has helped me tremendously."

Mr. Dube also has regular reflections with Gladys. The two of them have created a buddy system, sharing their goals and progress on a regular basis.

Creating and adhering to standard work was more difficult. But then Mr. Dube—who was not accustomed to spending time in the hospital units unless there was a problem—discovered that he enjoyed gemba visits. His hospital adopted a two-hour no-meeting zone every morning to keep people free for one-on-one status reports and gemba visits, and he steadily added to the time he spends in hospital units and work areas.

Once a week, he leads a "grand gemba" that includes all of his top executive team. An assistant takes minutes during the gemba so that they can review later with a written record. In addition, Mr. Dube does solo gemba walks twice a week. In this way, his standard work schedule filled out.

"The biggest magic for me has been in the way we practice humility: going to the front line to support, ask questions, remove barriers. People see that management is not a person who comes to reprimand or take them to task. They see support, and that has changed their attitudes," Mr. Dube says.

Just like Mr. Dube, Gladys added more gemba walks to her weekly schedule, and this has had a remarkable effect on her ability to be available to more people. With a daily management system in place to catch many issues on the front line early in the morning before they become full-blown problems, she is doing less emergency-response firefighting during the day. Instead, she can talk to the front line about ongoing issues—like compliance with handwashing protocols—and about team successes in their work.

Gladys has also been very intentional and open about her own behavioral goals. She tells people she is working on good listening skills and asks them to tell her if they do not feel heard. She has her radar chart hung on the wall, updated regularly, and encourages others to do the same.

There are many components to the success Mr. Dube and Gladys have been seeing in their hospitals. In one year, that neonatal unit with an 11.5 percent rate of hospital-acquired infections at its highest was able to slash the rate to 3 percent. The number of bacteria strains detected was reduced from 14 to 4. And their rate of preventable mortality dropped to 11.3 out of 1,000. Some of this was due to an inventive use of the housekeeping staff to become handwashing monitors. But mostly, this was about discipline—the discipline that people saw in their leaders, that their leaders asked, respectfully, of them. The goals are clear, visible, and revisited constantly.

REGULAR REFLECTION AND BEHAVIOR CHANGE

Kathy Krusie, who returned to the Midwest in 2015 and is now chief administrative officer of the provider enterprise for

Community Health Network in Indianapolis, Indiana, also hangs her behavioral goals on walls. She has included weekly reflection time in her standard work chart and marks that box with red or green dots when she fails or succeeds in keeping that date with herself.

"My reflection is two simple questions. What did I do this week that helped my team? What hindered my team? It has taken me a long time to get this practice on track," Kathy says. "But I've seen it help others, too. I am mentoring a couple of amazing young, energetic people here, and one of them was worried that, when pushed, she tended to respond too emotionally. So we talked about, instead of rushing from one meeting to the next, pausing to reflect on the next appointment, to prepare. This habit of reflecting helps us gain perspective. Now, I know that this is what I need to do in order to stay in a highly productive realm."

Reflection, leadership standard work, and regular gemba visits are not the only activities we recommend for establishing and practicing good behaviors, of course. But the stories told by Kathy, Gladys, and Mr. Dube offer some insight on how far a leader can go with these three simple activities.

We have also seen a very focused effort to promote behavioral change from our friend Eric Dickson, MD, CEO of UMass Memorial, whom you met in Chapter 2. Eric, if you recall, had inherited a situation that was short on trust and long on turmoil.

Even after operations began to stabilize and the organization was performing better on key metrics, staff attitudes and behaviors were often negative. "I've actually had to tell people that I was not able to hear a word they said because of the venom in their voice," Eric says.

Some of this can be attributed to being in Worcester (pronounced "woo-ster"), which is widely described as a city with a chip on its shoulder. Living in the shadow of nearby Boston, inhabited by flinty New Englanders, smiling at strangers was not encouraged.

"It can be a little rough and tumble here. There were times people felt just beat up after a meeting," Eric says. "And we would ask ourselves how we could turn it around. How do you call people on bad behavior? Do you confront them in a meeting? I'm not sure that's productive."

STANDARDS OF BEHAVIOR

First, Eric and his team decided, the organization needed standards for good behavior. So he and his top 15 leaders started talking about how they could establish key behavioral metrics, and then, how they could be tracked and improved.

Around this same time, a group of caregivers had begun talking to each other about how civility could be improved in the hospitals. Quietly at first, and then with more confidence, the group organized around the idea that they and their patients deserved a better environment. They wanted less rancor. They wanted respect and kindness. And since these were nurses, therapists, and physicians—people who believed in collecting data and being clear about their intentions—they wanted to clarify the problem.

Working on their own, and then with the support of HR, the frontline group surveyed thousands of people at various levels of the organization asking two simple fill-in-the-blank statements: "I feel respected when . . ." and "I feel disrespected when. . . . "

Survey data was then used by a team in HR to create an organization-wide understanding of what respect meant, how it could be observed, and how people could be held responsible. This work is described more fully in Chapter 6, but here, it is important to note that Eric's executive team took that frontline-generated project, saw its potential to change the culture, and elevated it to create change on a global scale.

When HR was on a path to use the new standards of respect as a training and awareness program, Eric pushed them to include an element of responsibility. He wanted people to actively work on changing their behaviors and to look to one another to assess how they were doing. Discussions between HR and executives yielded a path to do that: annual 360-degree feedback assessments for all managers.

"I wanted to move the needle on staff engagement and patient satisfaction, and I think this is one way to do it," Eric says.

Accountability is a term that many health systems shy away from, particularly when it comes to personal behaviors. Accountability can sound like a hammer in search of a nail. What we talk about instead is responsibility, which is more closely associated with trustworthiness. We are responsible for ourselves and to others. In this sense, responsibility can be a two-sided mirror, held up by every person with humility and respect. None of us is perfect. Self-reflection is necessary to gauge progress.

There are many ways to create those respectful mirrors. There is the large executive team in California whose members use group reflections, along with coaching, to both learn from and challenge each other as they strive to change their behaviors. There are 360-degree reviews, like the ones at UMass Memorial.

Probably the most straightforward way to get personalized feedback is to have a coach shadow a leader on regular gemba visits, team huddles, or other meetings. Coaches can be outsiders—and many health systems need that—or they can be trained members of the improvement team. In the long run, having trained and trusted in-house coaches is preferable because new leaders will always need this kind of help. More advanced teams can use the buddy system—inviting a trusted colleague to observe and offer feedback on actions and behaviors.

As coaches, we have developed a list of behavioral signals that we look for—simple signs to indicate that people are working toward their personal goals and being responsible to the group. For instance:

- *Willingness to change* can be observed by whether the person in question has an active discipline of self-reflection. That means taking time every week or every day to write down how people showed humility or curiosity this week, how they failed, and how they intend to change.
- *Humility* can be observed in the questions asked at gemba. Is the person asking *who* and *why*—which can be in invitation to shame and blame—or *how* and *what?* We are looking for those *how* and *what* questions, which show curiosity in the process.
- *Curiosity* is observed in whether a person is asking open-ended questions and asking follow-up questions—*how* and *what*—based on what the other person said, as well as carefully listening to others.
- *Perseverance* can be observed by the responsibility adopted by the person. Do people have a buddy or coach? Do they have a regular system of feedback built into their routines?
- *Self-discipline* is observed in standard work. Do people set aside some fraction of their weekly schedule to observe work, coach their team, or remove barriers for people to get their work done?

One other important note on the work at UMass Memorial is the distinction made between leadership behaviors and civility—a more generalized term. UMass sends out 13,000 civility surveys every year, asking medical students, interns, customers, and families about the atmosphere at the hospitals and clinics. They use the information to gauge the progress they have made, as an organization, toward better manners.

Civility takes place in shorter-term, transactional relationships. Even a deeply dysfunctional organization can maintain civility for short periods. Leadership traits and behaviors, however, are the fabric of organizational culture and end up being either tools or impediments to assist in problem solving.

"The two pillars for our work here are continuous improvement and respect for people. But if you think about it, most organizations have no way to measure that second pillar, or to know if they are improving or falling behind," Eric says. "We can change that."

Like the other leaders profiled here, Eric has positioned himself as a teacher and a coach. And like all of us, he stumbles off that path he has laid for himself on a regular basis. So, he uses a regular practice of self-reflection and works with a coach to keep himself on track.

In 2019, Eric was using an external coach, but he—like we—sees a more perfect future as one where health systems like UMass Memorial have in-house coaching capability for all levels of the organization. These coaching systems are rare, but they do exist.

Let's meet some.

Coaching

The primary job of a performance improvement officer is to coach the leaders of an organization, from the C-suite to frontline managers, to embrace and display the principle-driven behaviors that will guide improvement. And yes, that is a little different than the job description at most places.

In the two decades since the methods of the Toyota Production System first began migrating into healthcare, the job of the performance improvement (PI) office has been that of resident expert. Staffed with former manufacturing engineers who were learning healthcare and caregivers who were learning lean thinking (or any of its variations), the PI office was there to plan and lead rapid improvement events, teach people how to use the tools, and get results.

Teaching the tools and running events is still an important part of the job. It's just not nearly as important as coaching people on *how* they get those results. We know this now, after seeing and studying more than a hundred transformation attempts, because we have consistently seen that deployment of tools without the right intentions leads to marginalized and then dead-end efforts.

The initiatives that have real legs, on the other hand, consistently have leaders who focus on the cultural and behavioral aspects of transformation. These leaders know that how they communicate with others is just as important as what they say. These are traits that rarely come naturally, however.

People who pursue leadership positions usually value boldness, quickness, and having the right answer. Thinking about how their behavior affects people—and results—is not often in that profile. That's why they need coaching.

For many readers, this idea of PI officers as behavioral coaches to CEOs and CMOs will seem a far stretch. Will the PI director be welcomed into executive offices to talk about personal behaviors?

Fortunately, we have two terrific examples of organizations that have adopted the PI coaching model. There are many more health systems out there doing this kind of work—including some that have already been highlighted in this book—but these examples show two solid variations on the PI coaching structure that can serve as a template.

Carlos Scholz-Moreno, director of strategic initiatives for a large multispecialty physician group in Northern California (which prefers not to have its name published), has led the PI effort in two major health systems. He will give an inside look at setting up a coaching PI office from the ground up.

Didier Rabino, who helped lead the transformation of HealthEast in Minnesota and then stayed on as vice president and lean sensei when that health system was merged with the far larger Fairview Health Services, was trained in the classic Toyota Production System methods and brings that sensibility to the work.

Both leaders keep their PI offices small and focused on coaching and teaching. Their jobs are to spread the culture and knowledge of continuous improvement, they say, not to run events and update metrics.

Years ago, we advocated a larger PI office, based on the recommendations of John's first sensei. It was a common rule of thumb in manufacturing that the PI staff should equal approximately 1 percent of the organization's total FTEs[1] and be used as a training ground for the health system's future leaders. (Some consultants argued strenuously for an office equaling 3 percent of FTEs.)

In *Management on the Mend*, John highlighted organizations that had a lot of PI engineers, plus a steady stream of interns from the rest of the organization. These interns were rising leaders who took a 12- or 24-month rotation through the PI office to deeply learn the principles, tools, and behaviors.

These were valiant efforts but, in the end, cumbersome. If a health system had 700 managers, it would take decades to give all those managers a rotation through the PI office and provide the kind of in-depth training needed to transform the culture. Also, those larger PI offices led to the assumption that all those people on staff should be doing everyone's PI work: updating A3s, tracking various metrics, creating huddle boards. This was detrimental to spreading knowledge deeply through the organization.

---

1. FTE = full-time equivalent employee. An office with 10 full-time staffers and 6 part-time employees has 13 FTEs.

In that last book, John also showed Didier's method at HealthEast. The PI staff was small and focused on coaching leaders to conduct their own improvements. In the end, this was the model that proved most effective at spreading improvement knowledge and the right behaviors.

FINDING A COACH

We might not have met Didier had it not been for Kathryn Correia. The former president of hospitals at ThedaCare during its transformation, Kathryn arrived as CEO at HealthEast in 2012 determined to bring change to the culture as well as to the care processes. In her experience, the two could not be separated.

Early on, Kathryn took a couple of her new colleagues on a field trip to see what good looked like. At Andersen Windows in Menomonie, Wisconsin, they found it. On a walk through the plant's morning routine—with their huddles, their clear process for escalating problems, and safety checks—Kathryn saw a frontline operator uncover a problem and signal for help. Two local leaders immediately met the operator, asked respectful questions, and used PDSA thinking to contain the problem and begin root cause analysis to find corrective action.

"You can't fake that stuff," Kathryn said. "That was the culture we wanted."

So, Kathryn recruited the plant manager to HealthEast, and Didier—a former cabinet maker and engineer who studied with lean masters at Steelcase in Europe and Michigan before undertaking the transformation of Andersen Windows—began to learn healthcare.

Meanwhile, he was showing Kathryn a new way to think about the work of a performance improvement office. With a staff of less than 10 people, he began conducting workshops on A3 thinking, daily management, and strategy deployment for staff throughout the system. But instead of doing rapid improvement events for specific areas, he and his team coached leaders to run their own.

"When we had improvement workshops, our goal was to achieve business results, of course," Didier says. "But it was also to transfer knowledge. We had assessments after every workshop to find out what they learned, but we also were watching to see who was holding the marker at the end of the workshop. Were we still leading the group or did the local owner take over? That was our goal."

The PI office was also training apprentices—rising leaders in the organization who spent about 24 months in PI, learning to coach, use the tools, and lead workshops.[2] The apprentices would arrive in pairs and be assigned to one of the staff advisors—mostly engineers who came from manufacturing and had deep expertise in lean. In general, the apprentices would coach frontline leaders while Didier and the advisors would coach executives.

Executive coaching took on two forms. Didier coached the executive team as a group as they defined their common executive standard work, developed strategy deployment, and did the crucial work of deselecting initiatives. Strategy deployment is the system for ensuring that top breakthrough strategies, as defined by senior leaders, are understood and acted upon at all levels of the organization and that frontline staff know how their actions effect strategies. This can be accomplished through the daily management system, where people

---

2. Because the PI office was small, it did not have capacity for a large number of leader/apprentices. It was understood that these were a few cases and not the necessary path to advancement in the system.

in frontline huddles address issues such as safety (patient falls), quality (infection rates), and resource uses (staffing) identified by senior leaders. Strategy deployment is often tracked using an *x* matrix, described in more detail in Chapter 10.

Also, when executives were willing and interested, Didier and the PI advisors entered into more personal coaching relationships. The one-on-one coaching typically included 30- to 60-minute sessions featuring a few simple questions:

- What did you learn since we last met?
- Where do we stand now?
- Where do we want to be?
- How will we know we are heading in the right direction?

Executives used personal improvement A3s to focus their efforts on behavioral change. But most of Didier's coaching time with senior executives took place in the work.

"Our job, as I saw it, was to allow the leaders to be in specific conditions, experiencing real things," Didier says. "All of our beliefs are based on what we experience. So, we wanted them to have experiences while we were there to talk about it."

A CASE STUDY IN PERSONAL, ONE-ON-ONE COACHING

To illustrate his methods, Didier recalled an executive named Dave who led a very large chunk of the health system's business, revenue-wise, but who sometimes felt disconnected from the rest of the leadership team. Dave did not want to be left behind on this new direction for the organization, so he asked for personal coaching early.

Didier guided Dave to a self-assessment on 10 ideal behaviors. Dave identified two or three gaps between where he was and where he wanted to be and then set himself a goal to pursue excellence in visual management and self-discipline. Dave said he wanted to lead his team by example.

Knowing that leading with questions instead of answers was a core priority, Dave and Didier created a simple PDSA form that would help Dave ask for feedback from his team. Dave regularly asked his team members to rate his behaviors on a scale from one to five—rare, event-based, common, consistent, and uniform—and then used that information to guide his personal work.

"It was easy to see Dave's behaviors changing from one month to the next. He became one of our best leaders," Didier says. "And then, it was time to go further. He needed to lead from the gemba. So I asked him, what if we took his office away? Could he gather all the information he needed at gemba to make high-quality decisions?

"Dave turned around and asked his team that question. How could they make all necessary information visible? Dave's division was like a medium-sized business. He had a print shop, a legal office, sales. With his team, he identified where the information was located, decided how they would make it visible, and defined the routes to connect the locations."

Involving the frontline team was a revelation. Once they learned what was important to the senior leadership team, people became highly engaged in making that information transparent. The relationship between the front line and senior executives became more collaborative. A new type of teamwork emerged.

Not all coaching attempts were as successful, of course. Some leaders cannot give up the dream of power and control, no matter what words they say about humility and respect. This usually shows up in meetings or gemba walks when the leaders in question interrupt conversation about a problem or current condition with their own can't-fail solutions.

In the best-case scenario, the power brokers end up being surrounded by colleagues who remind them of the process preferred by the group. And if a coach is present in that meeting, he can respectfully ask, later on, how the power broker felt that his suggestions were received. Still, for a personal coaching relationship to work, a leader must be open and willing to change.

THE POWER OF GROUPS

Group coaching, especially in a structured setting like strategy deployment sessions, is a different matter. Because executives are accustomed to having a leader present options and guide them through material in strategy sessions, having a coach take that role is not so personally intrusive.

At HealthEast, and subsequently at Fairview, Didier employed a *kata*[3] type series of questions, commonly used at Toyota, to be sure that everyone was clear about the goals.[4] Using a flipchart and markers to make notes, Didier would ask the group:

1. What is our quantified target condition?
2. What is our current condition?
3. What are the obstacles that prevent us from achieving the target condition today? How do we know these are

---

3. *Kata* is a Japanese word meaning *form*, most commonly used to identify the choreographed training exercises for martial arts practitioners.
4. See Mike Rother's book *Toyota Kata* for a more complete illustration of these methods.

the real obstacles and that removing them will take us to the target condition?

4. What are the potential countermeasures to remove each obstacle? How do you know they will be effective? What are the potential adverse effects or risks associated with them?

5. Which one should we try first?

This was usually accomplished in several sessions with the senior executive and her team. A major goal of these sessions was always to deselect initiatives that were extraneous to the target state. After all, Didier says, it does not matter how well we work on the wrong problems.

Deselecting initiatives is, of course, one of the most difficult things a senior team does. Healthcare leaders are notoriously additive. There are so many worthy ideas for improving patient care and adding to our knowledge, it is hard to say that one idea is not worthy. But this is an issue of respect. Keeping the number of initiatives to a critical few shows respect for the time and stress levels of the people in an organization who will inevitably shoulder the burden of this extra work. And it shows respect for the initiatives that are selected. Keeping the number small means we want these efforts to succeed.

In California, where Carlos Scholz-Moreno was leading the transformation of a very large multispecialty physician group and coaching the executive team in strategy deployment, the path to deselection was in visual management. That means he used an *x* matrix with senior leadership. (See Chapter 10, on the *x* matrix, for an example.)

The *x* matrix offers at-a-glance information about the strategic initiatives in play, ranked by importance to goals, and identifies each initiative by its impact on True North. Initiatives are color-coded by the time and resources required to complete the work:

- A red dot indicates the work needs five or more hours per week.
- A blue dot means two to four hours.
- A green dot shows less than an hour of work required per initiative, per week.

It is a time-consuming document to put together and requires regular updating. But the x matrix is powerful because it clearly identifies the limitations of an organization's resources and serves as a constant reminder of these boundaries.

This helped Carlos guide his executive team—24 people with a lot of strong opinions—to create a manageable list of 10 mission-critical initiatives in active play. Waiting in the wings were another 11 initiatives deemed important and 7 more on a wait list. This is a big improvement over the 135 strategic initiatives that people were juggling when Carlos first arrived.

In the system Carlos helped set up, senior leaders had a steady, standardized cadence for managing strategic initiatives during their regular weekly meetings. Each initiative was reviewed monthly. Everything on the wait list was reconsidered quarterly. Leaders adopted strategic filters—a series of yes-or-no questions and observed conditions that created a decision tree, allowing leaders to prioritize initiatives—in order to deselect initiatives entirely or move wait-listed items up to active status.

Having a clearly defined process and visual management of strategy deployment helped make strategy meetings more productive, less rancorous. But the greater change lever, Carlos says, was the leadership-wide commitment to adopting and displaying the Shingo principles and behaviors and receiving regular coaching from Carlos and his group.

DROPPING ALL ASSUMPTIONS

Before Carlos arrived in California, he had already spent a number of years thinking about the role of a continuous improvement office. After years in manufacturing leadership—with companies that made underwear and then guitar strings—Carlos joined the largest municipal health system in the United States, New York City Health + Hospitals. Over the course of six years, he rose to become assistant vice president of process improvement.

Those were six years of sometimes-turbulent learning, and while there, Carlos led his group away from depending on rapid improvement events to focus instead on a daily management system and frontline problem solving. He had lived through the sugar high of big events and had landed in a very different place.

"The default way of thinking—tools get results—might get you there initially, but this only gives you the illusion of gaining control," Carlos says. "Really, you're creating a culture of compliance. Tools only answer the question *how*, but never answer *why*."

Arriving in California in late 2017, Carlos met the new health system's senior executive team, and what they really wanted to know was *how*? How will you get our continuous improvement efforts back on track? How will you fix our system? Carlos wanted everyone to take a step back, however, and ask some more foundational questions.

"We did an A3 on what our (PI) role should be in the organization. We started with very open questions to senior leaders like, 'What do you think we should do? How can we best help?'

The responses varied wildly," Carlos says. "Some people thought we should be updating their A3s. You know, doing all that lean stuff for them."

Senior leaders of this three-hospital, 10-clinic system had been working with lean consultants for about eight years. That work had been project based. The improvements they implemented stayed in pockets that shrank over time. The executive team recognized this and did not want to return to their old methods.

So, they agreed with Carlos—in theory—that they needed to change their leadership in order to change their processes. They decided to try coaching, but some remained wary—especially when Carlos laid out his plans to train his small PI staff to be the coaches.

"Some people said, 'No way. I'm a senior leader. I need someone super experienced.' We said, 'Look, we're always learning. We are learning to be good coaches. You are learning to be learners.' Finally, everyone agreed to a standard coaching schedule, once or twice a week, minimum," Carlos says.

This was a pivotal moment for Carlos. One of the hardest jobs facing any PI leader is building credibility with executive leaders. Most PI leaders did not go to medical school or earn advanced degrees in hospital administration. They are outsiders in the system, and it can be difficult for a CMO to consent to take instruction from a former manufacturing engineer. This is where an external coach—brought in specifically to help senior leaders grasp the idea of behavioral change—can be very useful.

BUILDING A TEAM OF COACHES

Also important here is a solid plan and process for conducting coaching in a respectful and effective way. Knowing this, Carlos started a new A3 with the following problem statement: We don't have a consistent coaching method.

As part of the countermeasures for that A3, Carlos and his PI staff created standardized coaching questions and schedules—a baseline that they could measure and judge as they went along.[5] He shared the schedule and coaching concept with executives and told them that he would ask for feedback every three months.

A group of six leaders in three model cells were assigned to coaches from Carlos's staff, under his oversight. Every coaching relationship began with clearly stated, standardized ground rules.

"We begin by asking, 'Do I have permission to be candid with you?'" Carlos says. "We need to develop trust. And it must be personalized, so we ask people how they like to learn—reading alone, for instance, or maybe by talking while being in the work—and how honest they really want to be. Because, if I'm completely honest, you might end up angry sometimes or frustrated. A leader might need to be told that their team members are afraid to be candid with them. That can be a hard conversation, so we need to talk about how to have those revelations come out."

Meanwhile, Carlos began personally coaching four C-suite executives. The team created a curriculum so that the executives would know, in advance, what their hour of coaching would look like, what they would learn and discuss. Everyone began with Carlos's idea of square one: True North and the principle *constancy of purpose*.

"After talking a little about what we mean by constancy of purpose and its importance, we have an initial reflection. We

---

5. Along with our colleague Tom Hartman, we assisted Carlos in this work.

ask, 'How do you, as a leader, create constancy of purpose? How do you communicate with your team, your direct reports, about what matters? When do you talk about performance? Show me in your calendar, where you practice constancy of purpose,'" Carlos says. "Normally, they are firefighting all over the place, so they can't really show constancy. That's OK. We can then start thinking about how to consistently communicate what matters."

At the end of the in-person coaching session, they also agreed on an activity to be observed. If a leader needed to better understand their role at gemba, it would be a gemba walk. If team dynamics were an issue, the coach sat in on meetings or status exchanges to observe. After the observations, they met again to discuss what the coach saw.

If the meeting being observed was a staff member's performance review, for instance, the coach would quietly observe, and then afterward, the coach would ask questions such as, How did you create a safe environment? How do you know that it's working? How do you collect information on performance?

In every case, the coaches would tell the leader in advance what questions they might ask in the follow-up interview. This became a very important point, Carlos says. "You don't want to catch leaders by surprise. They don't like that."

In addition to one-on-one coaching, the executive team also took up this work as a group. During the weekly executive team meeting, executives agreed to set aside 30 minutes for a group reflection, led by Carlos. He might ask how they understood constancy of purpose. How did they communicate it to others? Not everyone was willing to share at every meeting, but soon, conversations started.

Individually and as a group, for instance, executives looked at their calendars and began rating the meetings they attended each week. They found that not all of them were value added. Some meetings got eliminated; some were changed in content or scope.

And as executives created standardized work, they shared that, too. For every item of work, they showed themselves as green or red, for having succeeded or not. One of them might have a line item to check up on capital projects every week, for instance, or to practice asking open-ended questions, and there would be animated discussions about how they were earning a green dot for that work.

After 18 months of regular group reflections in the weekly executive meeting, senior leaders did not always need Carlos present to explain or referee. Sometimes, he stayed away on purpose to allow their reflection habit to be self-directed.

ANALYZING THE COACHING RELATIONSHIP

In the PI office, meanwhile, Carlos and his team created a process map of the coaching relationship. They met weekly to discuss who was deliberately practicing certain behaviors and how they could address gaps. They shared the questions they were asking, the problems their learners were encountering, and helped each other improve.

For each relationship, they set up a kind of PDSA for the coach to fill out, including notes on what the coach intended to achieve in the upcoming session, what the leader was learning, what the obstacles might be, what would be the focus of the next session, and how they intended to follow up. So, there were always two parallel lines of standard work being tracked: one for the learner, one for the coach.

In addition, Carlos was getting feedback from the learners every three months; he used that to tweak processes or redirect his coaches, as needed.

As the first year of this work was completed, Carlos had four coaches on staff, each of whom had four learners. They spent about 25 percent of the time coaching—about 10 hours of the week shadowing their learners or in one-on-one sessions. The rest of their time was spent in project management, training workshops, and facilitation of rapid improvement events.

"Rapid improvement events are necessary and will always be part of our system," Carlos says. "That's the way people learn the tools. But without a system to support the RIE, it won't last. It's not the tool that creates change; it's the behaviors."

As the first set of coaching relationships matured, there came greater demand. Executives identified new leaders that needed to deeply understand the work and, as usual, new executives joined the organization. The PI office needed to expand capacity.

So, Carlos set about hiring and training new coaches. He knew he needed five more people but started with two in order to experiment with training. He found people who had good technical knowledge and a few other traits he had identified.

"I knew we needed people with real self-awareness and strength in interpersonal relationships and problem solving," Carlos says. "They also need to be assertive, which is tricky because, as a coach, they can't be perceived as being pushy. They need to be unafraid to ask questions. So, not an accommodator and good with conflict resolution. We need collaborators, not competitors."

He figured his newly hired consultants would need six months of shadowing and learning. Carlos guided them through personal A3s and self-assessments. They created personal development plans; Carlos and the PI team leader did weekly status-exchange meetings with them on their progress. In those meetings, he would ask: What was your last experiment? What did you expect to have happen? What happened? And then they would show Carlos how they were applying the principles to their work.

With the rest of his PI staff, Carlos identified a series of markers that would show when the consultants—who were also conducting training workshops and helping to run improvement events—would be ready to take on solo coaching. He is still surprised that the new consultants passed their markers in three months instead of six and were ready to take on coaching relationships of their own. Within five months, Carlos was beginning to interview new candidates.

Another surprise: within about three months of beginning work with one of those new coaches, an executive learner sent back a note in his quarterly feedback form saying that his new coach was more useful to him than the super-experienced outside expert who was shadowing and supporting the coach.

IN COLLABORATION
WITH HR AND OD

One final note on this matter of a new role for the PI office that we have learned from long and sometimes painful experience: the PI office must move forward in partnership with either HR or organizational development (OD). Whichever office has taken on the mantle of training within the organization must be consulted. This should be a collaboration, although we understand that this can run up against executives who will treat change like a turf war.

In the best-case scenario, the HR or OD leader who oversees systemwide training will be one of the first executives to enter into the coaching relationship so that the leader can experience it firsthand. And if there are disagreements, they must be brought to the surface and given full consideration.

Too many times, both of us have allowed powerful executives to harbor silent disagreement. We have thought, "That person will come along, once they see the amazing results our teams can produce."

Leaders who remain on the outside of this work for too long can become resentful, however. And resentment is a hard spot to recover from. It is better to invite chief executives into a coaching relationship at the beginning—even if it is less formal—so that all leaders have the opportunity to see and understand the nature of continuous improvement.

One good method is to set clear timelines for each part of the organization to begin working in the steady cadences of a daily management system. To prepare each area, have executives receive coaching at the same time that frontline leaders undergo intensive training—often referred to as belt training—before the area makes the transition. In this way, each level of leadership can be receiving training and practice appropriate to their positions.

In Chapter 5, you will meet two organizations that found success with this rollout of the work. And in Chapter 6, on leadership in the support organizations such as HR, finance, and information technology, we will examine how good partnerships are formed across these boundaries.

First, let's meet some managers.

Frontline Leaders

Here is the worst thing an organization can do when trying to adopt principle-based behaviors: go to the managers and directors with a list of behaviors and say, "Here, do this."

It sounds tempting though, doesn't it?

After all, frontline management is where change initiatives have traditionally aimed their energies. The managers who supervise one unit and the directors who have a portfolio of units are an easy target. If they adopt a new idea and bring all their frontline caregivers and support staff with them, the pendulum will swing, right?

This plan has a couple of problems. The experienced managers will see you coming from a mile away with your sparkling new initiatives that (in their experience) do little but cause more work, and they will smile and duck. Some managers will be happy to try something new and, perhaps, imagine that being an early adopter will get them noticed and advance their careers. And then battle lines form between the skeptics and the cheerleaders, and a tremendous amount of energy gets wasted in this divide.

But the bigger problem with this plan is that it misses the point of behavioral change. For managers and directors, adopting these behaviors is not add-on work; it is the way they will get their new jobs done.

In a continuous improvement organization, the functional role of managers and directors is very different than in a traditional one. In most organizations, managers and directors were talented clinicians or frontline support. These people were organized, experienced, and energetic. They got promoted because they knew the work well enough to tell others how to do it, or to jump in and fix any issues that arose. They are conduits for orders from above, making sure that executive directives are followed.

But in a continuous improvement system, the job of managers and directors is to teach and coach their teams to become problem solvers. In this role, managers are not carrying out direct orders from above, and this can cause some anxiety. No longer can managers seek "the right answer" from a boss. Executives and other bosses are still responsible for guidance and direction, of course. They just don't have all the answers. Nor does the manager. The right answer to a problem is instead sought in the team's scientific thinking and careful problem solving.

The key traits we will be highlighting for managers— curiosity and perseverance—exist to support these talented, energetic people as they make a difficult transition from *doing* to *coaching*.

UMASS MEMORIAL:
IN THE CHILDREN'S UNIT

"We started this journey with an idea board that Eric [Dickson] suggested we put up on the unit in 2013," says Georgina Gardner, RN, manager of the pediatrics unit at UMass Memorial in Worcester, whom everyone calls Gina. "It was a dark time here. They had decreased bed capacity on the pediatric unit from 37 beds to 20. They were putting up walls and pushing us into a smaller area, and people would come to work feeling sick to their stomachs. In six months, the pediatric float pool was dissolved, and we lost all eight staff members.

"Still, we were going to start this huddle. We met at the idea board once a week, every Tuesday at 1:30. The mood on the unit was sad, though, and for the first six months, it was often just me and my physician partner, Neil Tyrell, at the meeting. We would ask people what they wanted done—anything—and then go do it," Gina says.

Gina and Neil had a coach from the UMass performance improvement office, and they knew it was not the ideal way to run a huddle—making little fixes and holding those lonely two-person meetings. But they were not going to force people to come, either. They wanted an atmosphere of respect. So, Gina took requests and then installed coat hooks, moved laundry hampers—just about anything people suggested.

When wait times in the pediatric ED got dangerously high due to a lack of beds to transfer patients into, the unit expanded again to 30 beds. And every Tuesday, she and Neil were there at the idea board, looking for things to fix. Eric, the CEO, showed up and asked if they had one wish, what it would be. They asked for more computers and got four new workstations on wheels, so the doctors no longer had to share computers with the nurses.

Tentatively at first, people started showing up to the Tuesday meeting with ideas and requests. Perseverance was paying off. Gina and Neil used some of that time in the huddle to talk about what they had learned about problem solving with an A3, and about looking upstream and downstream of a process to see what effects their solutions might have on other people—passing on the knowledge they learned from their coach.

More people attended the meeting; Gina went from acting manager to manager, and that same year, pediatrics was awarded innovator of the year for UMass Memorial, a distinction that came with a big cash award to work on an idea.

And then, just as Gina was reading more broadly about leading with respect and humility and preparing to start coursework for a doctorate in nursing practice, she received the results of the civility survey that UMass conducts every year of medical students, volunteers, and visitors. It was like a slap. In pediatrics, 60 percent of residents said they felt threatened in a conversation with staff; 46 percent said communication was poor.

"These were our residents. They were showing up and trying to do their best and they were feeling bullied," Gina says. "I had to look hard at how we behaved. Every year, we have something like a dozen new med students, interns, and residents show up to learn and work with us, and to be honest, I didn't even bother to learn their names. It was not uncommon to hear people talking badly about their own staff members. We seriously needed to change."

Gina took the survey results to the Tuesday huddle and presented them with a question: How could they address this problem? By this time, the pediatrics team was accustomed to thinking in terms of better engagement leading to better work processes and better patient outcomes. So they created an interdisciplinary work group and attacked the issue with interest.

Some ideas the team came up with were simple and quickly implemented. They began greeting each incoming group of medical students with ice-breaker games. They went bowling. They learned one another's names.

But then they needed to look at why medical students might feel bullied or get yelled at. They created a working group from the larger team to dig deeper into the issues. Sometimes, the group learned, tempers flared because mistakes were made or because the medical students seemed like they did not know simple things. A resident or intern would change something in a patient's room that should not be touched, or ask a patient or family questions that had been answered 10 minutes earlier. But whose fault was it that a medical student was in the dark?

It used to be that patient rounds—where each case was discussed and updated by caregivers—were conducted in a closed conference room and involved only physicians and a few nurses. Members of the working group asked each other, what would it look like if lots of people were privy to that information?

To include more people into vital information, the team in pediatrics moved the patient status reports to an open space at the nurses' station and invited medical students, therapists, pharmacists, social workers, psychiatric staff, and anyone else who needed to consult on patient care. Everyone was hearing the same information at the same time.

"We needed to change the mindset of staff, and that required structural changes to get us all working together," Gina says.

This work toward a more respectful environment was not just happening on the patient floors, either. Kathleen Hylka, director of strategic space planning at UMass Memorial, was selected to help roll out the Standards of Respect program.[1] An architect by training, she is detail oriented and thorough. She began her new role by googling "workplace respect" and reading everything she could find. Her leadership team decided that their first job—before they asked anything of anyone—would be to model the behavior.

"You have to be the change," Kathleen says. "Leaders need to walk the talk, and then they need to bring everyone along. Everyone. We can't say, 'Well, that person is the chair of such and such and brings in a lot of grant money every year, so he's allowed to be rude.'"

Members of the team were the subjects of some of the first Stepping Up Respect 360-degree reviews, which provided each person with feedback on three things they did well and three things they needed to work on. Then, each person created a personal plan with countermeasures to improve their behavior. Think of this as crowdsourced coaching.

"I got feedback on my first 360 review that it doesn't always seem like I'm paying attention to people when they talk to me. I'm a multitasker. So now, I close my computer when I'm talking to someone," Kathleen says. She admits that she is not scoring 100 percent on this action, but she's trying.

Back in pediatrics, focusing on the right behaviors and being more inclusive have had a significant impact. In 2019, three years after Gina was shocked by the civility survey results, her team had reason to celebrate. People who reported feeling threatened during a conversation with staff had dropped from 60 percent to 16.7 percent. And those who complained

---

1. A complete description of this program, with illustrations, follows in Chapter 6.

of poor communication dropped from 46 percent to 8 percent. Respondents who felt threatened by family members of patients actually rose a point, however, from 78 percent to 79 percent. So, the team has a new gap to address.

Here we should highlight two important elements of the behavioral change work at UMass Memorial that have enabled the spread of these ideas. First, it was led and modeled by leadership. Senior leaders determined what good behaviors were, specifically, and then modeled those behaviors and coached direct reports. If Eric Dickson had not been instrumental in setting up that first huddle board and attending the meeting in pediatrics to offer his help, the meetings might not have continued. Even in the months when it was just Gina and Neil at the board every Tuesday, it was leaders who were there, keeping the flame lit and inviting others to participate.

Second, UMass Memorial was also organized by a daily management system that acted like a kind of superhighway for ideas. In departments such as pediatrics and strategic space planning, leaders were consistently using team huddles and one-on-one coaching sessions to solve problems and discuss *how* the work was being done. There was a time and place to talk about respectful behaviors as part of the problem-solving process.

NATIONAL HEALTH SERVICE: USING THE DAILY MANAGEMENT SYSTEM

Across the Atlantic Ocean in Berkshire country—in England's southwest, home to Windsor Castle—the management team at Berkshire Healthcare NHS had also discovered that the management system was a natural conduit for behavioral change.

This is a community physical and mental health provider with several hospitals, about 100 clinics and 4,500 employees serving a population area of not quite a million souls. The system offers mental health care, treats learning disabilities in adults and children, specializes in dementia and memory care in the elderly, and offers home-based healthcare. It is a diverse portfolio with many sites spread over several towns.

Julian Emms, chief executive, began introducing the concepts of continuous improvement to Berkshire in 2017 with rapid improvement events. Very quickly, teams trying to implement change found that they had a hard time making improvements stick and decided to focus on a two-pronged strategy: implementing a daily improvement system to solve lots of problems at the front line, while also introducing and practicing principle-driven behaviors.

Senior leaders, in partnership with a local consulting company, developed training in A3 thinking, establishing standard work, and setting up and supporting huddles. Then they brought together leaders and introduced the principles of quality improvement—QI, in their vernacular—including leadership behaviors, how to coach others as they solved problems, and how to enable a culture of problem solving.

One of the people in those first training sessions was Rosemary Warne, a nurse consultant who was relatively new to Berkshire. She had decades of experience in clinical care, teaching, and leading projects, but she had not come across a management system quite like this before, where the quality improvement work was part of the work of day-to-day managing. It was unnerving at first. And then, it suddenly made sense.

"When the penny dropped for me, I incorporated more teaching into my regular work, helping others understand A3 thinking, huddles, standard work, and status reports,"

Rosemary says. Soon, she was named a clinical director, supervising and coaching the work of four matrons, who are each responsible for two ward managers.[2]

On units throughout the system, managers began using daily one-on-one status reports and team huddles to conduct their work. Problems uncovered in status reports were often addressed by the frontline teams, in daily huddles, where everyone was learning to use PDSA cycles and Shingo principles such as thinking systemically and assuring quality at the source to find local solutions.

Berkshire leaders also developed a clear escalation process for problems. When problems uncovered in a status report or huddle needed to be addressed fast or with additional resources, they were swiftly reported to the next level up in a clearly outlined manner. Meanwhile, strategic goals critical to Berkshire's True North were communicated down the chain of command. If top leadership chose to focus on patient falls as a quality metric, for instance, all units were asked to track and report on patient falls and daily status report meetings included questions about which patients might be at risk of falling.

Leaders like Rosemary all began developing standard work. Her calendar included attending one or two huddles on a unit every week, as well as regular gemba walks that she identified by subject matter. For instance, she would do safety walks with a ward manager to discover any lingering concerns at the front line of care. Rosemary would time staff walks to begin toward the end of a team huddle so she could connect with caregivers and listen to their experiences on the ward. Patient walks, likewise, were also about connecting with people and listening.

---

2. A ward manager is responsible for the work of a single unit. A matron in the United Kingdom is much like a director in the United States, supervising the work of multiple unit managers.

"I like the phrase 'Big ears, big eyes, small mouth.' When I am connecting with people, I really try to go without an agenda. I want to hear what they want to talk about," Rosemary says.

Like most of her leadership colleagues, however, many of Rosemary's days are consumed with meetings. Many of the meetings are good and useful, but there are too many to attend if one also wants to spend time at gemba, like Rosemary did.

So, she and a few colleagues worked out a schedule for attending some meetings in relay. One of their group would attend and type up meeting notes afterward for the others. The little bit of extra work for one meeting ended up freeing Rosemary from several others, adding hours to the week, which she can spend at gemba.

"I love going to a huddle and then staying behind after and chatting with people. Just by being open to a conversation to see where it goes, I hear things about safety and quality that I wouldn't otherwise," Rosemary says. "And really, I'm just making connections. I'm not in a QI role. I'm a clinical director using QI to do the job, which includes facilitating investigations into serious incidents. The more I know, the better."

Rosemary also changed the format of the monthly safety and quality meeting with matrons and ward managers, asking everyone to bring updated information about the countermeasures currently being implemented or tracked in their areas. This allows Rosemary a few minutes of coaching with everyone as they discuss the link between root causes and countermeasures.

And for the learning review panels[3] that follow a serious incident, Rosemary begins with a brief introduction that includes talking about the behaviors expected in that meeting.

---

3. These learning review panels are small, cross-functional teams that gather to investigate the circumstances around a serious incident involving safety or quality, look for root causes, and decide on next steps.

She offers a few ground rules and reminds people that they need to be curious, that the root cause answers they seek will be in the process, not the people.

"We're all working hard not to be reactive. We know that we don't need heroes. We need good, consistent processes. It's still a struggle for all of us, really," Rosemary says.

Another early adopter at Berkshire, Nikola Pollard, head of financial transformation, found that she needed to work at saying less in her huddles. An enthusiastic supporter of QI, Nikola was first introduced to organizational excellence 10 years ago and was in the first wave of green belt training[4] in 2017.

Immediately, she began advocating to overhaul the finance function at Berkshire, and she has been experimenting with getting rid of the old budget system in favor of rolling forecasts in two units.[5] At the same time, she began practicing daily status meetings with her own team and weekly huddles with the whole finance office—25 to 30 people—and all five of her fellow managers.

Not everyone was enthusiastic. Still, she pressed forward, quite certain that this was the right path.

"My management style involved a lot of telling rather than coaching. I needed to recognize when I was doing that. Now, instead of me talking through a ticket [an improvement idea or problem], I'm having people talk through their own," Nikola said.

To do this required some planning. Before a huddle, Nikola began looking at the improvement tickets to be discussed and then meeting individually with the authors. She talked them through their problem statement and asked the kind of

---

4. Green belt training is an introduction to the behaviors and tools of organizational excellence, and it is often given as a series of workshops culminating in student projects.

5. Rolling forecasts are described more fully in *Management on the Mend* (ThedaCare Center for Healthcare Value, 2015), pages 131–141.

questions that would likely come up in the huddle, helping the often nervous team member prepare to present.

During those prep sessions, Nikola was careful to ask open-ended questions instead of drilling the person on presentation. It was a slower process and did not always feel very productive, she admits.

"The coaching style felt really unnatural at first. Sometimes, I still find myself interrupting and directing and I check myself," Nikola says.

Becoming the coach she wanted to be was, Nikola knew, not a two-week endeavor. Sometimes her own ability to change seemed maddingly slow. Telling people what to do was so much quicker than listening and asking questions. But she kept at it because she knew that her real goal was even bigger—to break free of the constraints of her traditional role.

As a finance manager, Nikola was one of those people that operations managers love to hate, and who have considerable clout. All of the support functions—HR, IT, marketing, and finance—have people like this that they send out to do business with operations on a regular basis. The people from support services usually have closer contact with top leadership and are viewed as being the voice of "corporate." The power dynamic often leads to more private grumbling than open dialogue.

Leaders at Berkshire NHS had a different vision for this interaction. Support specialists like Nikola had expertise that could be of real value to operations. They just needed to speak the same language and have a common set of behavioral expectations.

So, Nikola was preparing not just to be a better leader in finance, but to be a partner to clinical teams and administrative offices—to assist anyone who could use the particular skills of a financial analyst. Let's see how that went.

Becoming Partners

Berkshire NHS is part of Great Britain's nationally funded health system, but its finance function is not so different from any other. Like most of its counterparts everywhere, the Berkshire finance team spent much of its time creating detailed annual budgets for the organization and all of its various divisions. Finance leaders analyzed the needs of units and clinics based on previous demand, allocated resources, and then tried to understand what went wrong.

They made budgets, argued about budgets, and audited compliance to budgets. It was never the most satisfying part of the job.

And so, in 2019, the finance team took its first running steps toward a very big leap. Before we follow them into that unknown, it is important to know a little bit about Berkshire and the people who would do such a thing.

Back in 2011, Berkshire NHS was solely a provider of mental health services.[1] It was well regarded and had good national ratings. Then the NHS decided that Berkshire should be merged with another healthcare trust—this one providing a range of services for the population's physical well-being, including home health care—and Berkshire leaders needed to reconsider how they were organized.

"It gave us the opportunity to really look at our organization and start reading broadly about organizational development," says Julian Emms, CEO. "We started using surveys to measure how people were engaged and to train managers more systematically. And because we were listening to people more, we started to fix some basic problems and gripes. We improved some of the physical conditions, upgraded IT where needed. We created some trust."

And then in 2015 came one of the big care-quality inspections by NHS. These used to happen every two or three years and were very disruptive—100 inspectors descending on an organization all at once, turning over every rock.

"We received a 'Good' outcome—a strong B rating—but it required a huge amount of effort beforehand," remembers CFO Alex Gild. "There was a lot of firefighting just before inspectors arrived. We dreaded the next inspection."

Discussions after this experience left leaders with two strong goals: to find a better way to improve at a steadier cadence and to earn that rating of Outstanding.

---

1. The NHS rates health trusts as Outstanding, Good, Requires Improvement, or Inadequate. Berkshire was rated Good.

Julian teamed up with the chief medical officer and chief nursing officer and began going to healthcare improvement conferences and touring health systems—such as Western Sussex NHS[2] and Virginia Mason in Seattle—looking for a path to improvement that seemed honest and sustainable. The three of them reported back to the rest of the executive team as they explored, and by the time that they were deciding to focus on organizational excellence, just about everyone was on board.

When they interviewed different consulting groups about partnering with them, the consultants faced a panel of about 100 people who were curious about how they were proposing to train and guide their people.

"The real pleasure of the journey for me was that we learned together. That was a privilege. From being introduced to something like leadership standard work to putting it in motion. We dedicated time to this—even whole days—to work with coaches together and alone," Julian says.

"Early on, we were all struck by how much work, how much time and effort were involved for all of us. People wondered how we could possibly do it all, and I listened and, well, I agreed. But we all worked it out time-wise because we knew we were working out a better system for everyone. Firefighting, you know, just takes too much time."

In many ways, Berkshire began in an enviable position. Leadership came from a common experience—that enormous effort preceding the quality inspection that resulted in a Good rating—and were unified in their goal to find a better way to

---

2. We had been working with the Western Sussex acute care health system for a couple of years at this point, and leadership was deeply engaged in improving its six major hospitals serving about a half million people. In October 2019, Western Sussex became the first NHS Foundation Trust to earn a rating of Outstanding in all six areas of quality review.

improve. They had a culture of working in teams and did not need to eradicate a lot of command-and-control behaviors.

Their goal, in fact, was even more unity. As they did the hard work of rearranging their schedules for coaching and gemba walks and huddles, and while learning to be responsible to one another as they practiced new behaviors, Alex Gild was keeping his eye on his big goal: aligning and integrating support services—and especially finance—with the clinical side.

"I really felt unsure that this could happen, frankly," Alex says. "Did the organization have line of sight back to our real goals? People didn't use our information. We're in a fast-paced environment, so I understand. I could see they didn't feel a strong ownership in the budget. It wasn't set by them. It wasn't necessarily useful."

Creating line-of-sight from operations to organizational goals began to happen as units huddled around moving the needle on performance metrics, discussing why certain kinds of improvement were emphasized. When senior leaders decided, for instance, to improve patient safety throughout Berkshire by eliminating patient falls, every unit and every huddle was talking about how they could keep their own patients from falling.

In status exchanges and huddles, they also discussed how resources were used and financial analysts helped teams understand and track business measures such as annual leave patterns and staff sickness, along with lagging indicators such as required hours of temporary staffing and the cost of different types of staffing. In time, clinical staff and financial analysts were speaking something very close to the same language.

For both operations and the finance department, however, the budget—with its annual batch of assumptions and rearward looking nature—was still a pain. Considering the direction of the rest of Berkshire, Alex thought, the budget was too top-down and inflexible. It did not accurately reflect the issues people were facing as they tried to set and achieve goals. In 2019, it was time to see if they could get rid of it.

BEYOND BUDGETING

Alex's goal was to replace the annual budget with a system of rolling forecasts and to transition every unit and department over with a program he called Beyond Budgeting. What is really noteworthy here is how he opted to begin this process.

Looking out over an annual budget report, it is easy to see that there are almost always units that struggle to manage their resources year over year. Frontline managers often take the blame, or extenuating circumstances are cited. But Alex decided to look at these units through A3 thinking. How could he and his team use root-cause analysis to better understand the issues at play?

"Our idea was to embed one of our finance managers in a unit to understand what was truly driving performance," Alex says. "So, for instance, Nikola spent six weeks working with an inpatient learning disabilities unit that had gone over budget by about half a million pounds every year. But we weren't there to understand why they couldn't stick to their budget. We were there to understand their needs."

Working with staff on the unit, Nikola helped them build a model of capacity and demand, which begins by determining the two or three key operational drivers of demand (patients) and capacity (staffing) and forecasting the impact of those drivers on required resources. Once the operational drivers were understood, they could create financial projections on a rolling basis.[3]

Using the capacity-and-demand model, it was soon clear that the unit had been choking on scarcity. Without enough full-time staff members on board, leaders were consistently forced to fill in the schedule with more expensive temporary caregivers from an agency. If the unit was allowed to hire two new staff members, they found, they could almost entirely stop using the agency and save at least 20 percent of labor costs.

THE ROLLING
QUARTERLY FORECAST

That does not mean they would be "in budget," however, because their budget was eliminated. In its place, Nikola helped them create a rolling forecast, which is an estimate of the unit's future needs, based on a deeper understanding of demand, updated quarterly.

Instead of imposing numbers on divisions and frontline units, finance managers would be helping unit managers create their quarterly forecasts of resources needed, rolling up those numbers into organizational forecasts, and then dispatching managers and accountants to help people that run into imbalances of capacity and demand. When gaps appear between target states and forecast, support-service personnel from finance, HR, IT, and QI would also be available to help unit managers improve.

Within the first six months of the beyond-budgeting experiments, Nikola did multiweek tours in podiatry and mental

---

3. Traditional budgeting environments typically feature a top-down allocation of fixed financial budgets not directly linked to operational drivers, which are therefore much less useful in describing current-state realities, let alone predicting future financial performance.

health inpatient services. She did not go so far as to move her desk and tea mug to those units, but she spent a lot of time there to understand their resources and demand. Then she helped managers create a forecast and left each unit liberated from its annual budget. And she became convinced that getting rid of all annual budgeting was entirely feasible.

More important, Nikola and Alex were changing the old conversation between operations and finance. Instead of beginning a meeting with clinic managers believing that they knew what the budget was—what the clinic "deserved"—they were going in with curiosity and humility, knowing that they needed to learn needs of that business.

Every unit that was introduced to the beyond-budgeting concept needed to have a daily management system—with regular status reports, daily huddles, and A3 problem solving to keep everyone focused on current conditions and root causes before solutions—to ensure that it had the QI maturity to ask the most relevant questions about its capacity and demand.

"This is a big change. But the benefit to the services is that they are getting resources released because we now have a much better understanding of what they really need," Alex says. "We are becoming better partners."

STEPPING UP THE
STANDARDS OF RESPECT

That desire for partnership often runs both ways, we have found. At Berkshire, change was initiated at the top. But at UMass Memorial Health Care, it was a staff-generated opportunity that led to partnership.

Remember that Standards of Respect initiative that was aimed at changing behaviors at the health system in Worcester, Massachusetts, the little city with a big chip on its shoulder? That actually began as a movement among caregivers that was embraced by HR as an opportunity to change the culture.

"This is a little embarrassing, because we knew that respect had been an issue with us, but the work really started with a nurse manager who was distraught about how she and others were treated," says Tod Wiesman, chief learning officer and VP of organizational people development. "She was pretty new here and was shocked at how people responded to conflict—at the language used and the rudeness."

Executives knew about the problem. Over the years, they had made attempts at fixing it. They wrote codes of behavior that nobody remembered. They tried to push standards but did not pass along a compelling argument for why anyone should change.

It was nurse manager Alicia Wierenga, finally, who said *enough*. She started talking about the problem with a few like-minded people. Their numbers grew to include physicians and therapists and others, and they began meeting to talk about how things should be and how they could get there. They started a movement.

"They did not want us in HR involved, at first," Tod remembers. "They did not want this to be a *corporate* thing. But finally, they allowed us to help a little."

What the group wanted was some compelling data, a starting point to make their case. So they created that simple, two-question survey on feelings of respect, filled buckets with candy and slips of paper with the questions, and offered people treats in return for answers. They got 2,300 responses and brought their findings to Tod for help analyzing the data. He found there was enough statistical significance in the answers to identify six major themes: listen, be kind, acknowledge, communicate, be responsive, and be a team player.

"A small group of us sat down and fleshed out the details of each standard based on those survey responses," says Laura Flynn, director of performance, learning, and education. "We knew that we needed to have training around this. But we didn't want it to be just about training. We needed a surround-sound approach."

By that, they meant a way to embed these ideals in everything from marketing to hiring and promotions. After so many years with inadequate solutions to an intractable problem, they wanted a moon shot.

CEO Eric Dickson wanted that moon shot, too. He told Tod and Laura and the team that he wanted them to present their biggest, best ideas for this Standards of Respect at a big executive meeting in February 2018.

For two months prior, Tod and Laura and others in HR cleared their desks and did little else than read, investigate, and plan how they could create awareness. They wanted a tool to help promote the concept, something tactile and memorable. They came up with a deck of 20 cards for the standards and the behaviors related to each, reminding people what it actually meant to be kind, to acknowledge, to truly listen:

- **Acknowledge.** Notice others and recognize their contributions or concerns.
- **Listen.** Give your full attention to show you understand and care about what others say.
- **Communicate.** Share appropriate information generously and as soon as possible.
- **Be responsive.** Respond in the expected time frame to show others' priorities are important to you, too.

- **Be a team player.** Do your work in a way that also helps others.
- **Be kind.** Choose to be friendly, patient, and compassionate—even when it's easier not to.

A sample of this card deck is shown in Figure 6.1.

FIGURE 6.1 **A Sample of the Standards of Respect Card Deck**

ADDING 360-DEGREE ASSESSMENTS FOR LEADERS AND MANAGERS

With their beautifully produced cards, their origin story, and a plan for rolling out a series of two-hour workshops across the organization, Tod and Laura went to the big executive meeting hoping for acceptance. What they got was an enthusiasm they had not bargained for.

"Dr. Dickson got up and said the standards should be more than just awareness training. We would also be including 360-degree assessments for leaders and managers," Laura recalled. "We did not know that would be happening."

The assessments would not be performance reviews, but a kind of plan-do-study-act (PDSA) cycle on the question of behaviors, they decided. Once a year, a manager or executive would select their review group, including a direct manager, a few peers, and a few people that report to them (Figure 6.2, see next page). Reviewers would answer a questionnaire detailing what three behaviors the person was getting right and three areas in which he or she might improve (Figure 6.3).

The leaders would then create a plan to strengthen their positives and improve in their areas of weakness. This opportunity for personal improvement added a level of responsibility that we believe should be present in every organization.

"We called it Stepping Up Respect, and it made sense to us because it's the people in leadership who are the models for behavior," Tod says. "Respect for people—that all-important pillar of our work here—can feel like a platitude without texture or teeth. We needed something like this to show that respect has equal importance with the second pillar, process improvement."

FIGURE 6.2 Stepping Up Respect: Manager Feedback. These are the questions to be answered by a manager's selected review group.

In the following areas, how should this person change his or her behavior or actions?	Do much less	Do less	Don't change	Do more	Do much more
Acknowledge					
1 Demonstrates gratitude (says thank you; comments positively on others' actions; recognizes good work)	○	○	○	○	○
2 Makes others a priority (shows personal interest in others; makes time for others; makes personal connections)	○	○	○	○	○
3 Honors diversity (is careful not to make assumptions based on appearance, name, gender, race, role, etc.)	○	○	○	○	○
Listen					
4 Gives full attention (stops other activities to focus on the speaker; stops using technology when others are talking)	○	○	○	○	○
5 Clarifies Understanding (summarizes or asks follow-up questions to ensure understanding of intended message)	○	○	○	○	○
6 Displays patience (pauses before responding; let's others finish speaking)	○	○	○	○	○
7 Seeks others' perspectives (asks if everyone was heard; invites others to speak; welcomes everyone's contribution)	○	○	○	○	○
Communicate					
8 Shares generously (provides all relevant and appropriate information; shares knowledge; shares the good, the bad, and the ugly; makes sure hand-offs are clear)	○	○	○	○	○
9 Confirms prior understanding (asks what others need to know before instructing/providing information)	○	○	○	○	○
10 Communicates considerately (uses simple language to aid others' understanding; uses best medium to share information, e.g., in-person, email, phone)	○	○	○	○	○
Be Responsive					
11 Shares updates (keeps people informed of progress; alerts others if deadlines are at risk)	○	○	○	○	○
12 Prioritizes the important (determines what's important and acts on it; is willing to delay less urgent tasks/items)	○	○	○	○	○
13 Delivers results (knows and meets deadlines; follows through on commitments)	○	○	○	○	○
Be a Team Player					
14 Is collaborative (commits to and acts upon shared goals; collaborates and/or cooperates whenever possible; brainstorms for solutions)	○	○	○	○	○
15 Helps others (says "yes" to requests for assistance; says what they can do, not just what they can't; proactively offers to help)	○	○	○	○	○
16 Helps others meet their goals (sets others up for success, e.g., next shift, teammates, other departments, etc.)	○	○	○	○	○
17 Considers others (shows up on time; shows care about how his/her work affects others)	○	○	○	○	○
Be Kind					
18 Displays empathy for others (recognizes and honors others' pain and joy; delivers bad news sensitively; comforts those who need it)	○	○	○	○	○
19 Manages own emotions (shields patients and families from irritation or frustration; displays patience under pressure; gives instructions and/or responds with a calm voice)	○	○	○	○	○
20 Is gracious (shares credit when things go right; takes ownership when things go wrong)	○	○	○	○	○
21 Intervenes for others (steps in when someone else is being treated unfairly or poorly; stands up for those that may need support or reinforcement)	○	○	○	○	○
Open-ended question					
1 What additional feedback, if any, would you provide to this manager?					

FIGURE 6.3 **Stepping Up Respect: Manager Feedback Report**

These are the three items identified across all raters as those you demonstrate well. Congratulation! Keep it going!

The three items you should continue demonstrating:

14	Prioritize the important (determine what's important and acts on it; is willing to delay less important task/items)
9	Shares generously (provides all relevant and appropriate information; shares knowledge; shares the good, the bad and the ugly; makes sure hand-offs are clear)
1	Greets people (is friendly; smiles and says hello; introduces self to others; uses peoples' names)

These are the top three items identified across all raters that are opportunities for improvement.

Your three priority items:

23	Manage owns emotions (shields patients and families from irritation or frustration; displays patience under pressure; gives Instructions and/or responds with a calm voice)
7	Displays patience (pauses before responding; lets others finish speaking)
19	Sets others up for success (next shift, teammates, other departments, etc.)

Source: Special thanks to CEO Eric Dickson for sharing his annual Stepping Up Respect review.

TRAINING WITH A VOLUNTEER CORPS

The HR team put a lot of research and thought into the training segment, too, creating a two-hour workshop that used a lot of humor and video clips to get the message across. There's always a lot of laughter coming out of those sessions, Laura reports, which is a good way to go into the written self-assessments that everyone does, looking at their own behavior.

In the first 18 months of the rollout, 400 workshops were held throughout the five acute care and community hospitals and six urgent care clinics of UMass. Approximately 10,000 caregivers had received the training as of the end of 2019, out of the total 14,000 employees.[4]

Putting on all those training sessions stretched the HR resources beyond capacity, so Tod and his team asked for volunteers to help lead the sessions. They ended up training 40 volunteers from throughout the organization to lead the workshops in teams of two, and most of those volunteers went on to give at least one training.

"I'm still pretty new here, and I can tell you it was highly unusual to see a grassroots initiative like this fully supported by leaders," says Jena Adams, a consultant in organizational and people development. "And it still feels grassroots in many ways."

PLANNING A PARTNERSHIP WITH STRATEGIC DEPLOYMENT

One more model of HR-operations partnership that is worth mentioning here comes from Sandra Geiger at Atrius Health, a

---

4. All employees are called caregivers, and the workshop was required for everyone.

nonprofit system of 31 multidisciplinary practices across central Massachusetts with 6,600 employees serving 745,000 patients. Less grassroots-driven than the work at UMass Memorial, it is a partnership model rooted in Sandra's expertise in *hoshin kanri*.[5]

A former physical therapist who became passionate about improving the patient experience at another large health system in Massachusetts, Sandra became VP of performance excellence there on the strength of her work leading the transformation of the ED. As she was working to spread the ideas of continuous improvement, however, the CEO of that health system retired, and a new CEO came in with a different direction in mind. It was a familiar story.

In 2017, the leadership team at Atrius Health—which had islands of excellence left over from earlier work with a consulting group—wanted help organizing their improvement work in a more holistic way and hired Sandra to assist in rebuilding their hoshin system and oversee operational transformation priorities.

Over the course of a year, Sandra worked with the senior executive team to create their True North measures, an *x* matrix with their mission-critical initiatives, and standardized work for regularly assessing their progress. Then, she worked with the eight major service lines—including obstetrics, internal medicine, and so on—to develop their hoshin initiatives, each with an *x* matrix that was linked to the senior executive team's priorities.[6]

Sandra also began teaching and supporting the daily management system to those that were interested, with an emphasis on local problem solving. Then the chief people officer—head

---

5. *Hoshin kanri* is the Japanese term for policy or strategy deployment—a consistent process to ensure that all levels of an organization are acting upon the strategic goals set by top leaders. While we usually use the term *strategy deployment*, here we honor Sandra's use of *hoshin*.

6. This is a three-level *hoshin kanri*, with interlinked *x* matrix planning: the senior executive hoshin is level zero; the major service lines are level one; and the support services such as HR and IT are level two.

of HR—left Atrius Health and Sandra was asked to apply for the job.

This was a $2 billion organization with more than 1,100 caregivers, and Sandra had never run a human resources organization. "But the CEO, Steven Strongwater, told me we already had skilled directors in the department with technical knowledge. What he wanted was a leader who could create partnerships within the organization, to strengthen the relationship between people and strategy," Sandra said.

Specifically, he wanted her to integrate the hoshin work of the executive leadership team and the service lines with critical HR functions and then supply the right training and assistance in the right areas.

Working with her directors in HR, Sandra led a reorganization of that department to break down some internal silos. And then she asked her directors to change their focus.

"Our most important customers in HR need to be the 400 organizational leaders of Atrius Health," Sandra says. "We need to understand their strategic needs and operational challenges and offer support and advice, where needed. Maybe it was in customized hiring plans, compensation, and incentives that support organizational objects, or in change management. We needed to be looking ahead, to offer early help and do it while modeling the right problem-solving behaviors."

In some cases, this meant carefully planned coaching. For instance, if one of the practices was preparing to change roles among the clinical staff—requiring some nurses to perform more hands-on patient care versus offering phone support, in order to create capacity for billing providers—then Sandra would want staff from Organizational Development involved early, consulting on how to manage change and be part of the work redesign.

But this kind of early intervention had not always been part of the HR approach. It was a new role for many. So, Sandra spent extra time with her HR leaders explaining the organizational hoshin objectives and how they played a role in helping to achieve it. She actively gave her people coaching support before they had crucial conversations because she knew that showing respect, humility, and curiosity would set the tone for the whole interaction.

As the hoshin director, Sandra could look across the organization's 11 x matrices and plan how to deploy the various types of expertise in HR to support the different strategies. In late 2019, she was seeing early signs of positive change as the service lines were beginning to reach out and ask for more specific help.

There are many talents in healthcare's support services that go wasted without solid, respectful partnerships. Too often, for instance, IT staff are thought of as software jockeys and data collectors, when they should be collaborating in the design of new patient care delivery. These are people who are trained to think in terms of information flow, and that is a powerful addition to a team. Yes, IT staff members also have insight into how any new care process will intersect with electronic medical records and how new ideas can be supported in the digital realm. But they also bring fresh perspectives and new habits of thinking to a team.

Likewise, marketing should be partnering with every leader that undertakes strategic planning. This is what marketing professionals were trained to do.

And the quality team—with its inside information on trends in bacteria contamination and hospital-acquired infections—should be assisting senior leadership in guiding the focus of the organization.

Partnerships are only possible by sheer luck—when the right people with friendly relationships fall into the right positions—or when everyone firmly believes in a set of agreed-upon leadership behaviors. Practicing these behaviors can be thought of as a shortcut to having a decades-long friendship built on trust and mutual respect.

Sometimes the glue that holds us together must be consciously made, practiced regularly, and come with system of responsibility to ensure that we remain the best versions of ourselves. It is not a failure to admit that we need this help.

Start Here:
The Assessment

How does an organization begin this kind of work, looking deeply at what drives its people and then asking individuals to change their behavior? How do we decide to take on new traits?

As with every systemic change, it should begin like an A3, with a statement of the problem and the current conditions. And this is the way we have found to document true current conditions: the assessment.

In this chapter, you will meet two very experienced practitioners and follow along as they perform organizational assessments to determine readiness for change. We begin this way to make it clear that there is no one right way to do it. Every organization is unique and responds to change—or the threat of change—differently. The assessment should bend a little to allow for local realities.

After having performed dozens of assessments, we offer a clear framework for what needs to be in an assessment and how the work of doing it should flow. Figure 7.1, later in this chapter, shows the outline we use in our Leadership Assessment. The assessment really should be done by an outsider, but this is not always possible. For organizations that do their own assessment, we invite you to use that outline to guide your investigation.

WHAT IS AN ASSESSMENT?

Let's dive in. An assessment is just as simple and as complex as any other current-conditions statement. It is the second item on a standard A3. The objectives and personalities involved can make it seem enormous in scope, however, because what usually needs to be assessed is how the top brass is leading and managing the work of transformation.

How do we know that the assessment will be scrutinizing executive leadership as opposed to, say, frontline managers? Let's look at the problem statement. In most health systems that have been trying to improve performance, the problem goes something like this:

- Improvements are not sustained over time.
- Areas of improvement remain isolated.
- There is little leadership involvement.

Boiled down, the problems are with organizational focus and lack of coordination, which are the responsibility of the C-suite. Executive leaders, therefore, must be involved from the beginning in a thorough, respectful assessment.

A leadership assessment can sound like we are inviting people to judge the effectiveness or likeability of individual leaders. We are not. The root cause of problems, after all, is almost always found in process, not people. We focus instead on evaluating leadership work processes and their behaviors within those processes. Are the desired behaviors already in place? Do the work processes support or undermine the right leadership behaviors?

In most cases, leaders will need to learn new ways to work and to begin acting their way into new behaviors. So, take care to depersonalize the word *behaviors*. The investigation is into work habits, not personalities.

Usually, the first task of an assessment is to go see the problem in its natural environment. Over the years, we have developed a good method for capturing the current state that we will show in this chapter. But it is not the only method, so let's take a look at the experiences of a few people and organizations who have done this work.

COURSE CHANGES AND FRESH INSIGHTS

For Carlos Scholz-Moreno—who has now led assessments on two large health systems—the problems were the same each time. "There were some terrific improvements in certain areas," he says. "But the work was not spreading to other areas and we couldn't sustain it."

Carlos's first assessment was at New York City Health + Hospitals, the largest municipal health system in the United States, where he was senior director of process improvement. The improvement team there had begun transformation efforts in 2008 with rapid improvement events and, after six years, had completed something like 1,000 events and could claim $343 million in combined savings and new revenue.[1] But improvements too often fell apart, and continuous improvement thinking was isolated in a core group of problem solvers.

So, the improvement team decided to implement a daily management system, beginning in four areas that worked as model cells. Remember, this is a huge organization with 11 acute care hospitals and more than 70 community health centers serving 1.2 million patients annually, so this was a very small beginning for the daily management system.

In each area, people created visual management boards and engaged in daily huddles; area CEOs performed regular gemba walks. People were trained in scientific problem solving, and managers learned to audit standardized work. Patient satisfaction scores jumped significantly in each area using the daily management system techniques.

Once those four areas were stabilized in the new work methods, the improvement team spread the daily management system. By the end of 2013, the system was installed in 15 hospital units or clinics, and senior leaders made plans to have the system up and running in 244 sites by the end of 2015. They were counting on viral enthusiasm and learn-do-teach training to help it spread.

While improvement team members were making plans to spread the system, however, it became clear that those 15 sites were struggling. Improvements fell apart. The sites were not delivering results on strategic initiatives. The VP of process improvement, Joanna Omi, Carlos, and a team of PI leaders

---

1. Kim Barnas, *Beyond Heroes* (ThedaCare Center for Healthcare Value, 2014), 155–156.

from throughout the organization put together a team and began an A3 with a problem statement that essentially said: We need to be able to respond to strategic priorities and we are struggling to meet the demands of the business.

And then team members went to the daily management system model cells and focused on asking open-ended questions about the experience of people on the front line.

"We would ask things like, 'What is valuable to you about the visual management board?' And we would hear things like, 'Nothing, really. You guys are the ones who care about the board.'" Carlos remembers.

"We would ask, 'How about the huddle?' And I can remember one nurse telling me, 'The huddle? I show up because I have to. But I've been trying to get a refrigerator to store my vaccines for the past year. Can you help me with that?' I realized they didn't even really have a path for solving their most important problems," Carlos recalls.

What was most disturbingly clear, Carlos remembers, is that the daily management system had become one more initiative—a whole series of things to do on top of everything else caregivers and their managers were expected to do in a day.

Together, Carlos and his team then reread *Beyond Heroes* and asked what they were doing wrong. It did not take long to see the pattern, he says.

"We basically had a manual for creating a daily management system—using RIEs, training the trainers to create the standards, etc.—and said, 'Do this.' We decided on the tool first and thought the tool would change behaviors. We had it completely backwards," Carlos said. "When the right behaviors for executives and senior leaders aren't displayed, new work might be sustained for a while because it is anchored in people's will to improve. But that will fade away when not enough attention is paid."

Instead of meeting in a daily huddle to review new data points on metrics chosen by others, people needed to come together every day to solve problems in pursuit of their principles: keep patients first, keep everyone safe, manage resources, keep learning, work together, and pursue excellence. If principles were driving the huddle, fixing problems like refrigeration for vaccines would always win out over reviewing metrics, Carlos reasoned.

So, Carlos and his team came up with a plan to flip the script, to have principles drive behaviors. (Joanna Omi retired during this work, and Carlos continued on as VP of process improvement.) They stopped working with their outside consultant and instead focused on creating support for addressing problems at the front line. They used working sessions in key areas to clearly define what mattered, resulting in systemwide principles and a list of expected behaviors for leaders, managers, and people at the front line.

Working through that A3 over 18 months—a project that included three weeklong rapid improvement events to create new systems—the team rebooted the daily management system in four key areas, including King's County Behavioral Health in Brooklyn.[2]

Focused now on frontline problems, the team at Behavioral Health, assisted by Carlos's PI team, used the daily management system to tackle issues such as reducing the amount of time a patient had to wait for an appointment. Over 16 months between 2016 and 2018—even while the hospital was moving from one electronic medical records system to another in what became a very disruptive process—people working in huddles and rapid

---

2. This had been the site of notorious quality-of-care issues in the past and was under Department of Justice oversight until early 2017 when a federal judge declared that NYCH+H had "exceeded expectations" in improved patient care at the site.

improvement events stayed focused on the issue and reduced the time to the third next-available appointment from 28 days to 4.

Getting that number down to a reasonable four days had far-reaching implications because it turns out that providers had been worried about continuity of care for their patients. If a patient was about to leave the hospital but needed care every week, and a provider saw that the next available appointment was three weeks out, the physician often kept the patient hospitalized longer. This was expensive and caused more slowdowns in the system. Once a patient could be guaranteed an appointment within days, fears dissipated and patients were released earlier. Beds were cleared for new patients, and getting care for a new patient in crisis became more reliable.

Teams fixed a few other broken links between inpatient and outpatient care and reduced the number of overstays[3] by 68 percent. This amounted to 59,200 fewer bed days over that 16 months and a savings of $2.9 million. At the same time, Behavioral Health's 30-day readmission rate dropped from 9 percent to 6 percent.[4]

ON ANOTHER COAST: FIVE AREAS OF INQUIRY

NYC Health + Hospitals is always undergoing reinvention. Top leadership is appointed by the mayor, and new administrations almost always brings in new people and ideas. As it was clear

---

3. The best practice was for patients to spend no longer than 15 days hospitalized. Anything longer was judged an overstay.

4. Kim Barnas, "Part of the Solution: Management Systems in Healthcare," Becker's Hospital Review, August 2018, https://www.beckershospitalreview.com/hospital-management-administration/part-of-the-solution-management-systems-in-healthcare.html.

that another such shift was happening, Carlos left New York for a large multispecialty physician group in Northern California in 2018.

Before taking the job as director of strategic initiatives in the physician group—a collection of two hospitals and 10 clinics and multispecialty offices—Carlos looked carefully at where leadership wanted to go in their improvement journey and saw a familiar story.

"They were passionate about improvement, you could see that," Carlos said of the leadership team. The group had been working with an outside consultant for eight years and implemented lots of improvements, but those improvements stayed in pockets and shrank over time. Nothing seemed to change on a fundamental level.

"They knew they were stuck and wanted to be unstuck. So they went looking for inspiration. They had gone to Seattle Children's, to Autoliv,[5] and they had come back with a few shiny objects—the concept of a house, visual boards, idea cards—but they were just tools," Carlos says.

As Carlos explained, "They also saw that leaders in those organizations acted differently. They were interested; they just didn't know how to change themselves."

Fresh from his experience in New York, Carlos believed that the organization needed two things immediately: agreement on their principles and an assessment to create a shared definition of their current state. Carlos and the 24 members of the leadership team decided "not to reinvent the wheel" and quickly adopted the principles first written by the Shingo Institute.

---

5. Autoliv is the world's largest supplier of automotive safety equipment; leaders there learned the Toyota Production System from leaders at Toyota Motor Corp in the 1980s. Autoliv is known internationally as one of the best examples of enterprise excellence.

Then they agreed to work through the assessment method we had been using with other organizations. It is a little more intricately woven than Carlos's open-ended questions of his first assessment, so let us walk through it with the California team (with gratitude that they were willing to share their experiences).

We have organized the assessment into five essential areas of inquiry:

1. Leadership involvement
2. Executive team behaviors
3. Organizational readiness
4. Teamwork
5. Respect for every individual

While questions within each category will vary based on the problems at hand, these categories have remained remarkably stable. We have found that these are the main drivers and predictors of organizational excellence.

1. Leadership Involvement

When we say leadership here, we are talking mostly about the system's senior leaders, including the chief executive. Because so much of healthcare has been reorganized in the last decade into multihospital health systems, this can include multiple hospital CEOs.

We have found that the most important questions to ask in documenting current conditions in leadership begin simply:

- Do leaders leave their offices?
- Are they comfortable talking to people on the floor (clinics, units, etc.)?

- If so, *how* are they talking?
- Is the leader curious and asking questions or giving directions?

As a benchmark, we look at whether senior executives are spending at least 20 percent of their time teaching and coaching, involved in improvement activities, or engaging in standardized work, such as a weekly or monthly assessment of projects directly related to True North.

For every assessment category, we ask the leaders to rate themselves from one to five. Then we spend time at gemba looking for evidence and offer an outsider's rating. For instance, an assessment category might be, "System leaders participate in four improvement activities per year as part of their management standard work and use questions that don't indicate an expected response."

A rating of one might indicate that the leader participated in one event. To earn a five, the leader would have to participate in four improvement teams per year and be coaching others in the practice of asking humble, open-ended questions.

The gap between how leaders rate themselves and how they are rated by outside observers is the starting point for a discussion about development. The goal of that discussion should be to create a plan—such as a personal A3 and, ultimately, an organizational transformation A3—to chart a course to close the gaps.

The California team did not have a CEO. Instead, the organization used a dyad in that position, consisting of the physician in chief and the medical group administrator for each location. The power-sharing model does not change the nature of the people who rose to leadership positions, however.

"Humility was hard," says Robert Azevedo, MD, physician in chief of the outpatient medical groups. "I was trained to solve problems, and I was really good at it. Now, I had to ask, how am I going to change the way I have led for the last 20 years? I wasn't sure I had the time or capacity for it."

A friendly guy with seemingly boundless energy, Rob loved the ideas behind organizational excellence and genuinely wanted to spend more time at gemba, helping others solve problems. When he looked at why his organization was unable to sustain improvements and then at the five desired behaviors, it all made sense, he said. If they—if *he*—showed more humility, curiosity, perseverance, self-discipline, and willingness to change, Rob was pretty confident he would change for the better.

He also agreed with the assessment report that he and his partners needed to do a better job developing the problem-solving capabilities of their direct reports. So, Rob worked out a personal development A3 with Carlos and signed up for regular coaching. He dedicated time to reflect every week about his interactions with others.

One of his biggest obstacles, Rob discovered, was learning how to stop giving "the answer."

"Let's say that leaders in the ED wanted to do [an improvement project] around patient flow. In the past, I would feel the urge to get in there and help them define the scope. I would say, 'You know, I spent a lot of time in the ED, so I think I know a little about flow.' That's how it would start," Rob said.

"Then, when I started trying to say, 'I don't know,' I would add things like, 'Ultimately, you're the ones doing the work. I will support you."

The words *I don't know* would not quite come out.

So, he would try again, saying, "This looks great. I don't understand it, but I am here to support you and I want to learn from you."

Those three words might still be missing from his reper-
toire, Rob will acknowledge with a laugh, but people could see
that his intention had changed. And that change, post assessment, was creating a new kind of dialogue.

2. Executive Behaviors

In this category, we ask whether hospital presidents, chief medical officers, chief nursing officers, and others at this level are
spending at least 40 percent of their time in deliberate practice of teaching, coaching, and mentoring. This includes time
at gemba, and also in various meetings. Are they providing
assistance and coaching others to effectively solve their own
problems, or are they providing solutions?[6]

Much of what we are looking for here is evidence that organizational principles are clearly stated and that those principles
are driving the right behaviors. When executives are leading
with humility, curiosity, and self-discipline, we will be able to
see it in how they talk to others, but also in how they organize
their time. Our most important questions here are:

- Are executives setting aside time to develop people, to
  participate in improvement activities, and to help create
  quality at the source?
- Are they open about their schedules and showing up to
  assist their teams?
- Do executives ask questions that indicate an expected
  response, or have they mastered the humble inquiry?

---

6. To rise to the level of *deliberate* practice, the executive needs to have clear intention, a thoughtful routine, and time to practice—preferably with a coach. In his
assessment, Carlos chose not to include a hard number like 40 percent.

3. Organizational Improvement

Updated and relevant visual management boards are one of the clearest signs that an organization is committed to improvement. Uniform displays and pretty lettering are not important. What we look for is current data, displayed in a place where people huddle daily, related to improvement projects and problem solving for that area.

Is work organized into value streams? Do people understand value streams and patient flow, or do these concepts only belong to the PI team members? We know that organizational excellence is sinking deep into the DNA of a team when people—both managers and frontline staff—understand value streams and use them to describe issues.

Are people comfortable talking about problems? This is one of the biggest cues to organizational readiness we see. Stand in a huddle and watch. Do people wince when problems are exposed, perhaps awaiting shame and blame, or are they coming up with a way to dig in and investigate?

Are patients invited to join improvement teams?

4. Teamwork

Problem solving by cross-functional teams is the root of every effort toward organizational excellence. If teams of doctors, pharmacy technicians, executives, and maintenance people can work together naturally and effectively, it is a good indicator of cultural readiness.

The question is, how many employees are invited and encouraged to join such teams? Are the goals identified as team goals, or are goals handed down from executives or a central improvement office?

The culture of teamwork can also be witnessed in how well teams respond to coaching and mentoring from managers. Is there an atmosphere of mutual respect here? Does being on a team afford people the opportunity to learn and grow? Do teams share their achievements, best practices, and breakthroughs across the organization?

5. Respect for Every Individual

The first benchmark in this category is a simple answer for those who conduct regular employee morale surveys: Is the organization enjoying increased employee morale? If it is not increasing, do you know why?

Respecting people means offering everyone the ability to learn and grow through formal training and engaging in a daily management practice.

Respect is also shown in how actively leaders pursue a safe working environment. Do accidents and near misses require an investigation with an A3 or similar problem-solving method?

Finally, we encourage organizations to look hard at promotions. If an organization tends to promote from within instead of hiring from the outside, it is a good indication of a robust training and mentoring culture.

The California team's most important realization came from answering the questions on leadership, which led them to create this problem statement: "Our leadership style creates confusion, opportunity for waste and prevents us from unleashing our staff's creativity and efficiency." And that is what led them to embrace coaching, and to deliberately learn and practice new behaviors.

There are many ways to assess the current condition of an organization, from the open-ended questions of Carlos's work at New York City Health + Hospitals to the reflection-and-feedback system of scoring that he used with the California group. Our next illustration, which occurred in Michigan, was more like the assessment we use at Catalysis, but with its own twist.

See Figure 7.1 (next page) for a full assessment.

ASSESSING A NEWLY FORMED HEALTH SYSTEM

When Al Pilong Jr. was asked to lead Munson Healthcare in Traverse City, Michigan, into a more cohesive system, he wondered how he would convince the leaders of eight other hospitals to adopt new thinking. As the CEO of Munson Medical Center, Al knew the pressures of running a big hospital with high aspirations. When a series of mergers and acquisitions created the new Munson Healthcare system with nine hospitals and dozens of clinics throughout northern Michigan, Al was named COO of the system and charged with making a sum of the parts.

The other CEOs, he knew, were all smart and committed to improvement. Teams in every hospital had all been engaged in some form of organizational excellence, working through problems with structured scientific thinking and creating standardized work processes at the front line. But they were all going about the work differently and with varied results.

The new entity, Munson Healthcare, was looking for solid improvements from every hospital. That was the commonality Al used to focus the team.

FIGURE 7.1 **Organizational Leadership Self-Assessment Questionnaire**

This questionnaire can be used to rate an organization's leadership. Rate the statements in sections 1 through 6 below on a scale of 1–4 as follows:

1. **Not started.** No continuous improvement program.

2. **Beginning.** Planning has begun, activities may have started, but no significant engagement and no significant progress.

3. **Growing pains.** Teaching, engaging, succeeding, struggling, and failing are all occurring as the teams make slow, steady, and sometimes painful progress forward. Leaders, physicians, and associates alike are becoming progressively more involved, more committed, and more capable of learning from both successes and failures.

4. **Sustaining.** The organization's principle-driven lean behaviors can be described as teaching, mentoring, supporting, encouraging, enabling, humbling, steady, predictable, teachable, engaged, committed, and disciplined. Cultural behaviors drive many successes and also occasional failures with A3 thinking (or an equivalent structured problem-solving method) being applied in all cases.

1. System Top Management Engagement

1.1. The board you primarily work with is supportive of the organizational commitment to lean.

2. Local Organization Top Management Engagement

2.1. Organization leaders are all competent lean leaders, spending at least 40 percent of their time teaching, coaching, and mentoring the organization.

2.2. Organization leaders participate in one improvement activity each week with VPs participating daily as part of their management standard work.

2.3. The organization has a strategy deployment process that connects the breakthrough strategies to the frontline work.

2.4. Lean competence is a requirement for managerial promotion.

2.5. Principles drive behavior to the extent that these principles are clearly observable as cultural traits. Note: these behaviors should be evident in the daily work and service that is provided to the patients.

2.6. Organization leaders fulfill their role as lean leaders by leading some improvement events and participating regularly in improvement activities.

3. Commitment to Improvement

3.1. The organization embraces the pursuit of perfect service, quality, and patient satisfaction, understanding that this will also progressively reduce cost.

3.2. Organizational leadership understands that improvement is essential to the fulfillment of its mission.

3.3. There is no "blame and shame" environment so it is safe to expose problems.

3.4. Patients join with team members in improvement activities to support and accelerate the rate of improvement.

3.5. Continuous improvement is a powerful source of personal satisfaction for providers, caregivers, support staff, and top management.

4. Teamwork

4.1. Cross-functional teams (including providers, caregivers, and support staff) operate naturally and effectively.

4.2. Employees are trained in team building and are encouraged to participate in lean improvement activities.

4.3. All goals are identified as team goals encouraging each team member to engage in both goal development and execution.

4.4. Teams respond well to management coaching and mentoring with significant team initiative and capability being demonstrated.

4.5. Team-driven improvements result in the achievement of team goals with associated sharing of best practices.

(continued)

FIGURE 7.1 **Organizational Leadership Self-Assessment Questionnaire** *continued*

5. Respect Every Individual

5.1. The organization is enjoying increased employee morale.

5.2. Senior leaders focus on raising the skill and ability of providers, caregivers, and support staff through formal training and the daily management process.

5.3. Senior leaders show respect for providers, caregivers, and support staff, keeping them safe from harm with accidents and near misses requiring an A3 (or equivalent structured problem-solving method).

5.4. Resources that are no longer required for reacting to problems are redeployed to proactive roles, thereby accelerating improvement.

5.5. Promotions from within the organization demonstrate managerial commitment to the organizational culture, instead of hiring from the outside.

6. New Care Model Development

6.1. Organizational leaders understand and support the need for the development of new care models.

6.2. There is a culture of innovation where leaders have patience for development, teams take appropriate risks, and new services are created regularly.

6.3. Strategy deployment clearly lays out challenging goals around the development of new care models.

6.4. Resources that are outside of operations are dedicated for the purpose of developing new care models.

6.5. A robust and repeatable care model development process that is separate from daily improvement processes continually delivers new care models into operations.

"In the first meetings with all the CEOs, we talked about how we drive results to get to our goals. They were open to trying new ideas because everyone was on the hook to show results in their hospital," Al remembers. "For me, how we got to the results was just as important as getting those results, so we went through an iterative process, defining our True North and then identifying our principles and behaviors."

When the team had finished that work, it was time to assess where they were in their journey. This was carried out in two parts:

1. First, leaders rated themselves on issues such as whether their behaviors reflected Munson's principles, whether leaders actively participated in improvement activities, and if there was evidence of standardized work for leaders.

2. Then, two knowledgeable outsiders came in with a list of the same questions leaders had used to rate themselves. They spent a day in various hospitals and units, watching interactions and conducting interviews. Later, the team met again to confront the gaps between what they believed and what outsiders observed.

"For me, the results were a surprise. We weren't as far along as I thought we should be," Al says. "We had been doing lean, PDSA, and other approaches in all the hospitals. Every leader had their own idea about how to create improvement and we thought that would be all right. But in the assessment, we clearly saw the confusion and extra work we were causing due to the lack of standards.

"And the other big revelation was that we had too many initiatives happening at once. We kind of knew that we were suffering from overcommitment. But having evidence right in front of us was a big moment. We had to recognize that over-burdening our people was not respectful."

Using True North as a guide, the leadership team whittled down the list of initiatives and then each CEO created a personal A3 to track their growth.

When making a personal commitment to change, we all need some external form of responsibility to keep us on track. In leadership teams, we always suggest that the members are responsible to each other. And the team at Munson came up with a very smart way to do that, which they referred to as status exchanges.

Whenever they had regular planning and strategy meetings, they set a timer. They spent 30 to 40 minutes on operations, 15 minutes on strategy, and 15 minutes reporting on personal development.

Knowing that they would be expected to report on progress of their personal A3s made them more likely to look hard at where they were and where they intended to be.

"The hardest thing for me was to take time for the personal reflection that is required," Al says. "I'm pretty hard driving and activity focused. But I owed it to my team to report on how I was doing. So I had to carve out 30 minutes every Friday—I put it on my calendar—to write in a journal about certain events during the week, how I handled situations, and how that behavior reflected our principles. That habit came in really handy, as far as remembering what happened and how I wanted to be. Finally, I could see change occur over time."

Al used the idea of status exchanges as he taught his direct reports to use personal A3s, as well, thus ensuring that mentoring was part of his regular routine of meetings.

Without the original assessment that showed leaders where they needed to change in order to support organizational improvement, would Al have known that he owed it to his team to take time out for personal reflection? It probably would not have occurred to him. Al wanted to do well, but without the mirror of an assessment, it is difficult to know where to begin.

It is difficult for any of us to know where to begin change until we know where we are.

In the next section of this book, we describe some of the instruments we use to see where we are in greater detail. If learning by reading how-to is not useful for you, feel free to skip to the final section on work that is in development now.

All eyes are on the future of healthcare. This work will be crucial in the years ahead.

PART II

Instruments

The Personal A3

Throughout this book, we have highlighted the power of the personal A3 to help leaders identify and focus on behavioral changes they need to make. It is the first step in a leader's personal transformation. Figure 8.1 (see next page) is a sample (blank) A3 Personal Improvement form; this is also available as a download at catalysis.org/personal-A3.

Before we go into detail about how to use a personal A3, however, we should clear up one misconception. The personal A3 is not a problem-solving tool like the standard A3. A leader's behavior is not a problem to be solved.

Yet, all of us can improve. Our hypothesis is that leadership behavior is a condition in the workplace. This means that it must be considered as a factor in operations, and therefore, it is open to improvement. Because this is sensitive territory, we obviously cannot set up a team to study the issue and propose solutions.

FIGURE 8.1 A3 Personal Improvement

Personal Improvement A3 Title:

Date:
Authored by:
Coach:

Background
Why should I improve myself in order to be a coach / leader who creates an organization filled with problem solvers? Why this, why now?

Current State
Habits / Actions I Currently Take → Outcomes From My Current Habits / Actions
(Strengths and Limitations)

Opportunity Statement -1 Concise Sentence

Goals / Targets
New Desired Condition. What does better look like for me? What, How Much, By When?

Analysis
Reasons for My Personal Performance/ for My Current Strong Habits and Limiting (Gap) Habits

Proposed Countermeasures
What experiments will I try on myself to become a better coach / leader of problem solvers?

Plan / Next Steps
What steps will I take and when? What is my practice plan to develop new habits?

Follow Up
How will I know if there's improvement?
How will I know if things are off plan?
How will I make time to practice?
What is my process for ongoing reflection / P-D-C-A?
Who else will I involve?

144

Instead, we have leaders use the personal A3 as a method to encourage evidence-based thinking about their leadership. It is a framework for identifying goals, gaps, experiments, and plans for intentional follow-through. It has the same sections as a regular A3 and is iterative in its use.

It is designed to help leaders focus on their strengths and opportunities, to create personal responsibility, and to gauge progress toward their goals. And really, everyone in this work has the same goal: to create an organization filled with problem solvers.

Those who adopt an intentional practice with the personal A3 begin by acknowledging two facts. Leadership behavior has an outsized impact on the motivation and attitudes of people in the organization, intentionally or not. And nobody has a perfect understanding of the effect they have on others. In doing the work of a personal A3, leaders learn to see more clearly how they are facilitating change—toward becoming that organization of problem solvers—and how they are getting in the way.

We are all doing a little of both.

Developed by Margie Hagene[1] and based upon John Shook's book *Managing to Learn*, the personal A3's power is in the way that it draws a clear connection from individual behavior to organizational goals, even while keeping the work of individual growth very personal. It has proven so useful over about a decade since its introduction that we begin all leadership coaching relationships with it.

Please note that we draw a clear distinction between a person's traits and behaviors. A trait is defined as a summary of a person's qualities. For instance, we might call a person *bold*.

---

1. A former global internal consultant for Ford Motor Co. focused on transformation and organizational effectiveness, Margie Hagene is now on faculty at Catalysis and the Lean Enterprise Institute where she coaches leaders in a variety of fields.

A behavior is the specific evidence of that trait, such as out-spokenness for the bold. So, when we talk about behaviors, we are focused on what can be shown by the evidence. Instead of saying a leader is or is not humble, we are interested in seeing evidence of humility when working through a personal A3.

In the following pages, we will step through each section of the personal A3 as a coach would—asking questions, warning of pitfalls. While every person and situation is different, there are enough commonalities, we believe, for this to be useful.

TITLE

The title of an A3 should not be an afterthought. You are about to devote some significant time and personal energy to this endeavor. What are you trying to accomplish? The title should tell us—and remind you—what will be the focus of your thinking.

It can be as simple as "My Improvement Plan," or "Becoming a Better Leader for Problem Solvers."

A title can also provide a clear indication that you are heading in the wrong direction, particularly when the title focuses more on the organization than the individual. Titles such as "Getting Physicians Engaged in Improvement" or "Creating More Productive Meetings" are clear indications that a leader is moving the focus away from the self and onto the organization.

Certainly, physician engagement and more productive meetings are worthy of an A3 in many organizations. But those are problem-solving A3s. This is a personal A3, and we need to focus here on personal gaps and strengths in order to get at the root of more subtle issues.

If you have titled your personal A3 with an organizational goal—or skipped that part—and come back to these words later, this is an opportunity to reset. Dig a little deeper. Why are you putting in the time for yourself?

This may also be time to find a coach, a person whose job it is to help you pay attention to how you approach this work. Over the past decade, we have found that nearly everyone needs a person like a coach or facilitator to bounce ideas off of and to challenge the usual ways of thinking. We need to be encouraged to push beyond our initial instincts and to stay personal, to be willing to change ourselves instead of trying to change others or our organizational structures.

DATE

Write down a fresh date every time you do another iteration of work on your personal A3. No more than one or two months should pass between sessions, particularly during your early practice with the personal A3. There will be new assessments to make, changes to be noted. If more than three months have gone by, more current evidence of what is working and what is not will be lost.

AUTHOR

That's you.

COACH

This is usually an outside professional or a trusted colleague with experience in the discipline of keeping the work personal, intentional, and respectful.

BACKGROUND

What is the nature of this issue?

Perhaps you have noticed that nurses do not linger when you stop to chat. You explain this away by saying that people are busy, that your leadership position makes a lot of people shy. Still, you wonder about the pattern.

Maybe you are annoyed with the way meetings go. Resolutions are elusive. Your fellow leaders continue lobbying for a particular solution or point of view long after the official meeting breaks up. The conversations seem endless, and yet the executive team is not having the kind of honest, fierce discussions that you need.

Or, maybe you haven't seen the surface of your desk in two years and it seems like the tasks pile up much faster than anyone could handle.

These are good starting points when thinking about the background of your personal A3. Everyone has these vague, indistinct issues. Investigating these patterns is how we identify our gaps.

If we were to attack these issues with a traditional A3, we would probably end up focusing on the nurses, or on the other executives, or the way work is distributed as the source of the problem. What is wrong with them? How can we change the process that is causing this problem?

The personal A3 opens up the possibility that your behavior is helping to create these situations. For instance, maybe you tend to pontificate instead of asking questions and that makes people less inclined to open a conversation with you. Or maybe you have a tendency to impatiently cut off debate too soon in team meetings. Do you prefer to do the work yourself rather than teaching and coaching others?

Two more important questions to consider: Why is change needed? What would be the consequences or risks of not participating in the change? If you do not articulate for yourself the reasons for self-improvement and the probable repercussions of inaction, it will be too easy to remain in stasis.

The personal A3 will help you identify the root of the issues, but only if you let it. Therefore, begin broad with the nature of the possible problem. And then be clear about why you seek improvement and what the consequences might be of ignoring it. We need these personal reminders as to why the work is important.

CURRENT STATE

Begin this section by listing the specific actions you have already taken to commit to this exploration and the outcomes of those actions.

Perhaps you have talked with colleagues about the impact of your behaviors, or—hopefully—you have completed a radar chart to assess your strengths and limitations. (See Chapter 9 for a deep dive into radar charts.) Review the specific evidence collected thus far.

Data collection remains an important part of the A3 work, but it looks different here. Questions and answers from personal reflection are important data points. A radar chart is also valuable data. A lunchtime conversation with a trusted insider can be a rich vein of information and insight.

An excellent source of data is to do a poll of peers, bosses, and subordinates asking that they identify your strengths and stumbles. Good questions on such a poll might be:

- What have you observed in my behavior that unleashes creativity in others?

- What specific behaviors of mine have shut the team down?

Many people will be tempted to use annual performance reviews as data inputs. This should be avoided. In most organizations, performance reviews are little more than the opinions of one person crammed into a check-the-box format. They are required pieces of paperwork and usually lacking in generous insight. The performance review does not ask how a person could improve; it asks if the person is good enough to do the job at hand. It is the wrong question.

The critical takeaway here is that you need to collect evidence of how other people view your actions and note those alongside your own thinking. Do they connect? Are you focusing on the right issues?

Remember, the work here is to identify your strengths as well as your limiting behaviors.

OPPORTUNITY STATEMENT

The opportunity statement is a product of your own deep reflection; nobody else can suggest one for you. For those of us who avoid deep reflection, this can be uncomfortable. It would be far more efficient to select one from a list of prompts, right? Pick the opportunity that sounds most achievable and move on.

But this could only offer a vague and probably meaningless direction. Nobody wants to spend months chasing a vague and meaningless direction. Only you will recognize the grains of truth in the feedback you get from colleagues.

For instance, when Al Pilong Jr. was first introduced to this work, he was prepared to undertake some real action. Al was comfortable with action. But the CEO of Munson Medical Center and COO of the newly compiled Munson Healthcare got feedback that he was already doing a lot. Too much, perhaps. His opportunity statement was a simple realization: I would rather *do* than coach others to do.

For Mr. Dube in South Africa, feedback from colleagues made him see that most people only saw him in firefighting mode. Deeper reflection led him to realize that he was not that comfortable being out at the front line without an immediate job. His opportunity: Go see in order to understand. (As opposed to go see in order to fix.)

Note that, in each case, the opportunity was personal. This is where it is particularly tempting to shift focus to the organization. That's where the problem is, right?

Focus on this as an opportunity for you.

GOALS/TARGETS

The goal is not perfection. You, a human being, are aiming for better, not perfect.

The first step toward defining this better state is personal reflection. You probably know what better would feel like. Now, you need to translate those feelings into actions—into observable, measurable behaviors.

This is often the moment where people need to go back and reassess the current state, because the goal also needs to be meaningful to the situation and to the people that will be most affected. It needs to stay personal.

For instance, Al's target state was one in which he coached others to solve problems instead of taking tasks from others. But coaching was not the only goal. Al wanted to be an *effective* coach and to instill problem-solving capabilities in people throughout the organization.

So here, in his reflection on his target state, Al was also thinking about how he could measure his coaching effectiveness, such as tracking how many problems got solved before they hit his desk.

Mr. Dube's goal was to find ways to be comfortable at gemba—observing, listening—when there were no fires to fight or tasks to accomplish. That means he needed to work through some discomfort, which was a sign he was heading in the right direction. Discomfort almost always points toward a gap to be addressed.

Like a great many CEOs, Mr. Dube was more comfortable in his office—where people came to him—than at gemba. Working in this way, the conversation about the problem was almost always being held far away from the work itself. It was not ideal.

As we dug into the reasons for his discomfort, it became clear that Mr. Dube's gap was that he had not clearly identified his purpose at gemba. He needed to arm himself with humble questions and to reflect on what he wanted to learn from others. Soon, he was enjoying his time at gemba, where he felt more effective than he had in his office.

With these two examples, you can see how goals are tied to opportunity statements without being overly reactive. The target state does not expect organization-wide changes; it does not expect others to necessarily change their behavior.

Instead, we create personal goals that can be observed by others, intentionally monitored by us, and reflected upon in order to better understand how individual behavior effects the whole organization.

ANALYSIS

Why are you acting this way?

We do not want to go down a rabbit hole of childhood disappointments or Freudian analysis here, but this is an important moment of reflection on root cause. You need to ask why and how you began to blurt the "right" answer or try to control situations or whatever the issue is. Only when we understand why we behave in a certain way will we see how to make intentional changes in a way that make us feel comfortable and valued.

Many clinicians can trace some of their undesirable behaviors to medical school, where they were taught to make clear decisions, inform the team, and maintain control of the situation. Or maybe you came up through the leadership ranks based on your knowledge and good ideas. After years of getting good notice and promotions based on your ability to come up with solutions, it is natural to have difficulty giving up this role.

Understanding why you act the way you do will help illuminate your gaps and, from there, guide you to the next steps and experiments.

Al Pilong, for instance, knew that he felt good when he solved problems for others. He felt like an asset to the organization. How could he feel valued without doing that?

In his target state, Al envisioned a future where he taught others and coached them as they solved problems. This was another way to help people and be an asset to the organization, he knew. A root cause contributing to the gap was that he did not feel entirely comfortable becoming a teacher. Like many people, he had not acquired the teaching/coaching skill set.

Analysis leads to the plan.

PROPOSED COUNTERMEASURES

This is a simple list of experiments to try in order to become a better coach and leader. Maybe you want to learn to ask better questions. A countermeasure might be taking a list of effective questions (see Figure 9.2 in Chapter 9) with you to gemba and check off the questions you asked. It might be taking a colleague to lunch and practicing asking those questions naturally.

This is simply a list of actions that directly relate to your opportunity statement and your gaps.

PLAN/NEXT STEPS

Like a problem-solving A3, this step in the process has many parts: identifying experiments, developing a plan, checking the results of those experiments, and making adjustments based on outcomes. Add to this a practice plan, which is simply a detailed plan for practicing new behaviors every day.

For a leader who needs to better understand frontline operations, or who needs to learn to observe without offering opinions, the practice plan might be a regular series of gemba visits with a coach or colleague to observe.

For someone like Al, who needed to teach and coach others, the plan would include acquiring some teaching skills and then adding regular coaching sessions into his schedule.

To stay on track with the personal nature of this work, we advise people to stick to "I" statements when describing their plans. This should be familiar territory for anyone who has undergone interpersonal communication training. For instance:

- "I will go to gemba and ask only open-ended questions."

- "I will talk less and listen more."
- "I will learn how to ask open-ended questions."
- "I will update my radar chart monthly."

Create a clear start date for the experiment being run and list exactly what you will do and when. Make sure it is clear how you will know that the experiment is being run.

FOLLOW UP

After creating a plan and schedule, ask how you will know if you are improving.

Most people build time into their schedule for personal reflection, to ask if they are doing the work and whether they are noticing a difference. Maybe people are responding to you more openly? How do you know that? Note specific instances.

You need specific feedback from others, such as a coach or trusted colleague. Also, ask for opinions from the people in your regular huddle or committee meeting. It can be unnerving to be so vulnerable, but this is also an excellent example for others. A CEO who goes into a meeting and announces that she is working on her listening skills and asks for the group's help by raising a hand if she interrupts or runs over someone will have a roomful of helpers. And she will be living evidence of the seriousness of behavior change and her commitment to this work.

Another type of feedback we regularly employ involves one-on-one interviews with just one or two scripted questions. In this exercise, the leader might say, "I am working on my own personal improvement, and I would like your help in evaluating my progress for my A3. Can you take a minute to answer two questions for me?"

Take notes either while people reply or just after this interview in order to freshly capture their words. Many of us emphasize either the positive or the negative so strongly, it can be difficult to remember nuances of what another person says.

Once the evidence begins to show that your behavior is indeed changing, it will be time to return to the section on current conditions. Has your behavior change achieved the desired effect? If it has, how will you continue this practice? If not, what are the new experiments you will try?

Do not forget self-reflection. We are our own best critics; reflection is the path to improvement.

Which is why—up next—the radar chart is so powerful.

Your Radar Chart

The purpose of a radar chart is twofold. We use it to turn vague thoughts and feelings into measurable data and then to track progress toward a goal over time. Figure 9.1 (see next page) shows a sample radar chart; this is also available as a download at www.createvalue.org/radar-chart.

With periods of regular reflection in front of their radar charts, leaders are able to identify gaps and intentionally change specific behaviors. In this way, what can be a frustrating exercise—understanding our progress toward personal growth—becomes both visual and productive.

Kim has a good example of this from her own improvement work. Regular reflections in front of her radar chart made her notice that her score for curiosity was stubbornly low. She wanted to work on that and thought about the behaviors that show evidence of curiosity—especially asking questions and

FIGURE 9.1 **Radar Chart**

effective listening. While Kim knew she *was* curious, she realized that she often hesitated before asking questions because she wanted to be sure of her wording. Too often, the right moment for a question would pass by.

In her office, Kim had a large chart with a list of good, open-ended questions to ask at gemba (see Figure 9.2). Wouldn't it be nice if those were close at hand when she was at gemba? So, Kim took a picture of the questions with her phone and started taking a moment before she walked out on the floor to review the questions.

John likes to describe questions as gifts we offer to others. The right question at the right time can spark a whole new outlook on a situation, leaving the other person empowered to see problems in a new light. As Kim reviewed her list of questions, thinking about the people and the work she was about to see, she became more eager to find just the right one. Instead of asking a question to get information, Kim started thinking in terms of what the question could offer the other person. Not

FIGURE 9.2 **Sample Effective Questions**

1. What is the problem you are trying to solve?

2. How would you describe what is happening as opposed to what should be happening?

3. What have you looked at or heard about?

4. What makes you sure you have a cause/effect link?

5. What have you thought of trying?

6. What impact do you expect that countermeasure to have?

7. What makes that so important?

8. What might you do to figure out _____ about _____ (patient, customer, vendor etc.)?

9. How do you learn about that?

10. What process do we have to facilitate that discussion with _____?

11. Tell me more about what you mean when you say _____?

12. What would be an exception to that?

13. What is the definition of _____?

14. How do you set that up and present it?

15. What do you know about _____?

16. How do you know we're not doing that?

17. What does good look like today?

18. How do we know what they want?

19. How do you determine demand?

20. How do you know cause and effect?

21. Who have you spoken to about this?

22. What do you know about that?

23. Tell me one thing you think about that.

24. What evidence do you have so far?

25. What impact does that have on _____?

26. What improvements have occurred so far?

(continued)

FIGURE 9.2 **Sample Effective Questions** *continued*

27. Describe the obstacles to _____?

28. What was the outcome?

29. So where does it break down?

30. How could you show that visually in your A3?

31. That sounds like a solution—lets go back to the left side.

32. What have we learned from _____ about navigating that?

33. Who currently owns that process?

34. Who are the stakeholders?

35. How will you explain that to them?

36. What are the other scenarios that might happen if you deliver that message?

37. What factors contribute to this?

38. How was that decision made?

39. How do you know there is variation?

only did she begin asking more questions, more confidently, she felt better about the exchanges she was having.

In this way, the radar chart can be used to inspire improvement goals, as well as being a source of data for the current-state section on personal A3s.

USING THE RADAR CHART

Our radar chart always has the same five leadership traits and eight supporting behaviors. We have seen this chart work well for leaders and organizations from San Francisco to South Africa.

To fill out the chart, take note of the indicators for each level. This is how you score your actions over time. Every level, 1 through 5, is defined by how frequently you engage in the behavior, how long you spend in the activity, and the intensity of your focus:

- Level 1: rare, undeveloped, indifferent
- Level 2: irregular, experimental, apparent
- Level 3: frequent, predictable, moderate
- Level 4: consistent, stable, persistent
- Level 5: uniform, mature, tenacious

For Kim to reach Level 4 on her curiosity trait, for instance, she would need to judge her questions, answers, and A3 thinking as consistent, stable, and persistent. While her questions were irregular, experimental, and just barely apparent to others, she could not get past Level 2.

Every leader who completes a radar chart looks for where the line pulls in toward the center. This is the visual indicator of a gap—an area in which to focus improvement efforts. Figure 9.3 (see next page) shows an example. Here you can see that the leader scored high in "asking questions" and low in "effective listening." So, it is quite clear where a disconnect is occurring.

In three or six months, when you reassess and create a new radar chart, it will almost certainly look different. Maybe you will have improved in some areas but have not been able to get to gemba as much as you would like, or you recognize that responding to urgent situations has sent your leadership standard work schedule into disarray. Fluctuations in the chart are the result of paying attention to how you spend your time.

If you take notes during daily or weekly reflections, these can be very useful to review before updating your chart. And regular updates will help you see patterns over time.

FIGURE 9.3 **Radar Chart with Scores**

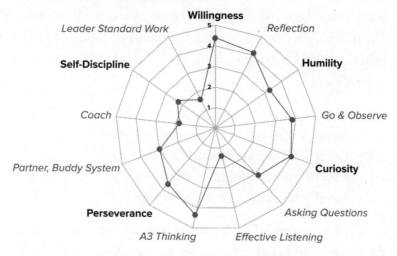

The real work here is deep, honest self-reflection. Take your improvement efforts where the evidence leads you.

DEFINING TRAITS AND BEHAVIORS

Following are explanations of the traits examined in a radar chart.

Willingness to Change

Willingness to change, highlighted in Figure 9.4, is at the top of the radar chart because transformation is only possible when leaders are willing to change. It is ground zero—or high noon—of the necessary traits. If we accept the premise that leaders model behavioral expectations for the organization, then leaders must be willing to change, to learn, to think differently, and to behave differently.

FIGURE 9.4 **Willingness Wedge**

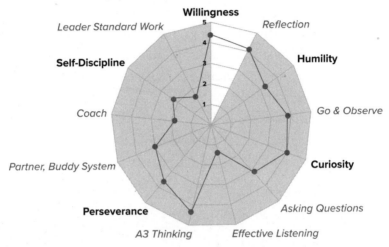

Observable Behavior: Reflection

Reflection is the practice of giving serious thought or consideration to a specific topic in an intentional manner. Reflection assumes that a leader carves out time in a busy calendar and brings depth and purpose to this activity. Some people find that asking two simple questions at the end of every day is necessary to establish the habit. Reflection queries in this case are usually simple, such as:

- What did I do that unleashed the creativity of my team?
- What did I do that shut my team down?

Other leaders can only manage one reflection a week. The key here is constancy. Setting aside time to think deeply about personal change is a clear indicator of willingness to change.

Humility

Humility, highlighted in Figure 9.5, can be defined as the condition of having awareness of your limits and, therefore, knowing that you do not know everything. Humility is an enabler for those who seek to learn the truth. Without humility, learning would be unnecessary. Humility assists us in shifting our self-perception from knower to learner.

FIGURE 9.5 **Humility Wedge**

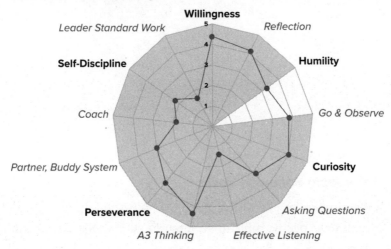

Observable Behavior: Going to Gemba to See, Listen, and Learn

Go & observe is to publicly embrace the knowledge that you do not know—cannot know—everything. It is a way of telling your organization that knowledge is more important than authority. Those who go to gemba to pontificate, or to tell people the "right" way to complete a task, may feel the sugar high of power, but they undermine the real purpose of the visit. You cannot learn while giving instructions.

Curiosity

Curiosity, highlighted in Figure 9.6, is defined as having a keen interest in how things work. It is the state of being inquisitive, of showing the desire to learn. Leaders who are curious ask great questions and regularly seek the views of other people. One positive implication of leadership curiosity is seeing solutions emerge from the front lines more than new programs launched from leadership offices.

FIGURE 9.6 **Curiosity Wedge**

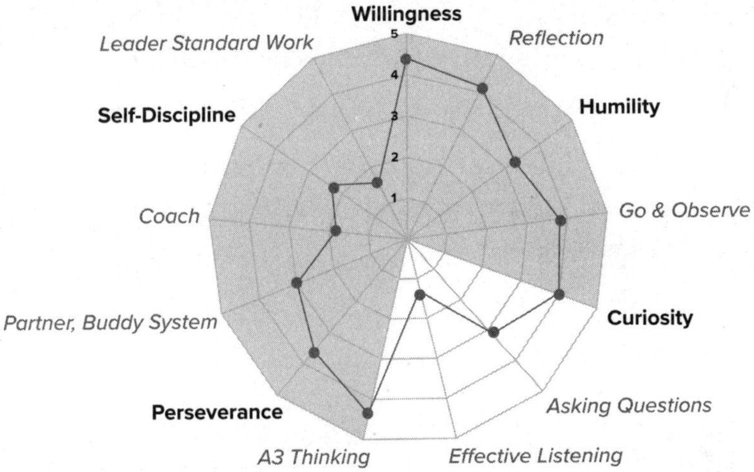

Observable Behavior: Asking Questions

Asking questions is the art of drawing another person out. The persons on the receiving end of questions should feel valued, safe to share their thoughts, and like a meaningful contributor to the organization. Do not ask questions to which you already know the answer. Do not try to guide others to the answer you have in mind. Other people almost always know your true intention.

Observable Behavior: Effective Listening

Effective listening is to give full and complete attention to another. Like the right question, it is a gift to give to another. By listening with empathy and without interruptions or solutions, you set the stage to allow others to find their own answers. Quietly preparing to say something during a conversation is not the same as listening.

Observable Behavior: A3 Thinking

A3 thinking is really just a way to describe organized curiosity. An A3 is an investigation into vexing questions such as:

- What is hindering that team from hitting their targets?
- Or, why is there always a long waiting list for appointments in dermatology?

Done well, an A3 helps to create a space that encourages curiosity as people discover their own answers.

Perseverance

Perseverance, highlighted in Figure 9.7, is persistence in the face of difficulty. Perseverance is not allowing a bad day to get you down. You may be coming back to the same personal development issue time and again, but this allows for the search into deeper understanding and new insights. This is what is required for personal development over time. Perseverance demands a certain psychological hardiness, but the good news is that practicing perseverance reinforces that same psychological resilience.

FIGURE 9.7 **Perseverance Wedge**

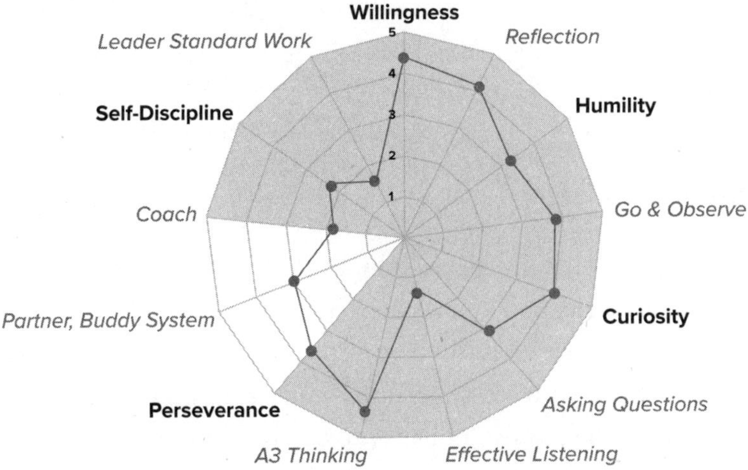

Observable Behavior: A Partner or Buddy

Partnering or a buddy system is a source of support when times get rough, when doubt creeps in or old habits resurface. Partnering is also an indication that you are willing to let others in, to share your journey. A buddy can be a trusted colleague, an outside mentor, or an internal PI facilitator, but it should be someone you trust. This will be the person who understands your development goals and creates a system of friendly responsibility.

Observable Behavior: A Coach

Having a coach, whether internal or external to your organization, work with you to create a leadership development plan and then challenge you, helps you create responsibility and acts as a sounding board. Many executives already have coaches for other purposes. Only use the same person for this purpose if they are deeply experienced in organizational excellence. In most cases, you will need another person to guide and facilitate your path to personal growth. This should be a fairly short-term arrangement. Our coaching engagements usually last 13 to 15 months.

The learning journey lasts a lifetime, but the intensive coaching period should be limited.

Self-Discipline

Self-discipline, highlighted in Figure 9.8, is the continual regulation and correction of one's behaviors. It is required if personal growth is to be sustained. The challenge for senior executives here is to move from conceptual understanding to personal practice of the important behaviors. Self-discipline is required to develop and reflect on the leader standard work necessary to keep you on track. Questions for this reflection include:

- How am I doing?
- Did I achieve the number of gemba visits I planned for the month?
- Did I get feedback from my buddy on the type of questions I asked at gemba?

Self-discipline is the trait necessary to keep consistent.

FIGURE 9.8 **Self-Discipline Wedge**

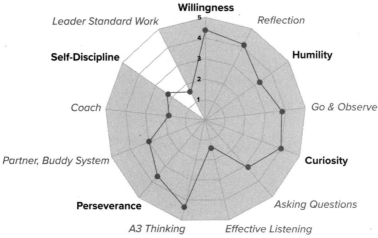

Observable Behavior: Leader Standard Work

Leader standard work establishes the platform upon which to practice and improve. It is a scientific fact that you cannot make improvements upon an unstable platform. Standard work provides the stable platform that allows people to truly assess their effectiveness, create experiments to change areas in which they are underperforming, and improve over time.

Leader standard work is personal. But there is also leadership *team* standard work. The following chapter describes how leaders will align and deploy strategy together. Spoiler alert: self-discipline is required.

The *X* Matrix
for Strategy

To organize, prioritize, and track the work of an organization's most important strategic initiatives, we use an *x* matrix that is specific to this purpose. This is a living document, an iterative method for focusing on top strategic priorities, deselecting less-than-critical projects, and keeping the work aligned with the resources at hand. It is separate from the way in which we consider and prioritize operational initiatives and only comes into play after the leadership team has completed its strategic development process. Figure 10.1 (see next page) shows an example. A downloadable template is available at www.createvalue.org /x-matrix.

FIGURE 10.1 **X Matrix**

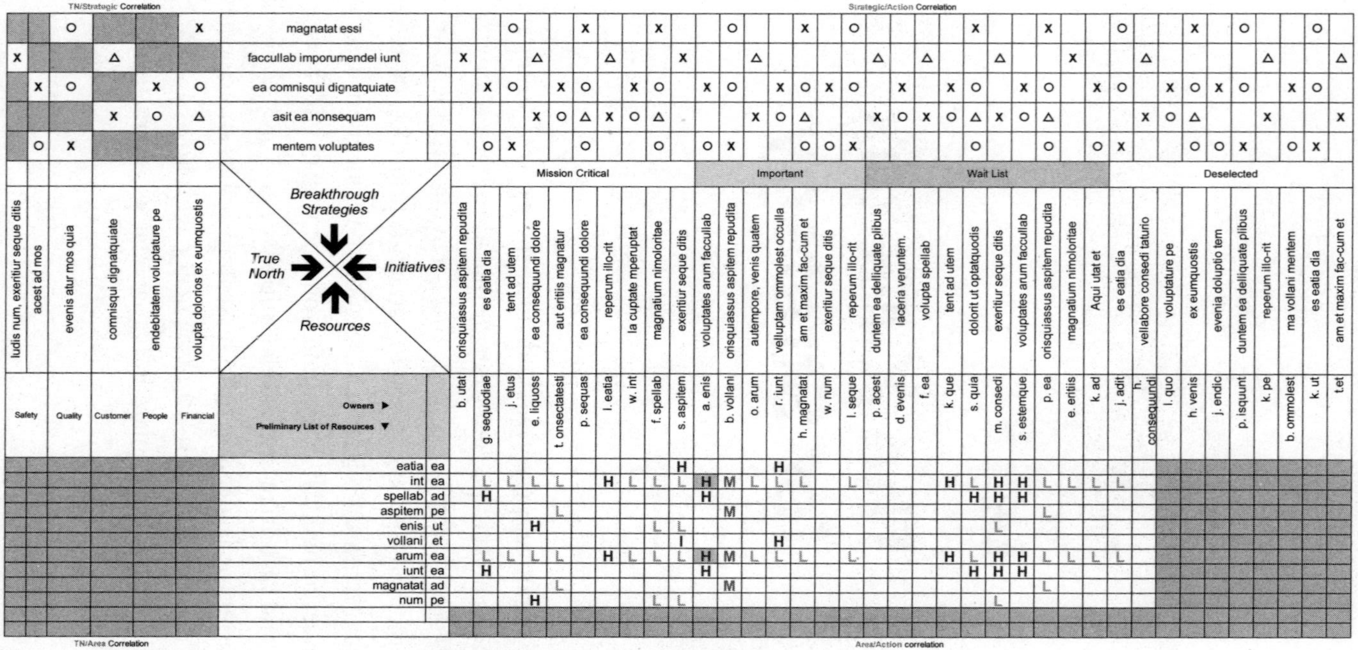

FIGURE 10.1 **X Matrix**

TN/Strategic Correlation

TN/Area Correlation

Strategic-Action Correlation

Area-Action correlation

Breakthrough Strategies

Initiatives

True North

Resources

Owners ▲
Preliminary List of Resources ▶

Mission Critical

Important

Wait List

Deselected

×	= Strong correlation - High Impact
O	= Important correlation - Moderate Impact
△	= Weak correlation or Low Impact

H	HIGH
M	MEDIUM
L	LOW

H	= 5+ hrs per week
M	= 2-4 hrs per week
L	= <= 1 hr per week

| H | M | |
If shaded, additional resources are needed.

172

The first time working through an *x* matrix is time intensive and requires a deep understanding of each breakthrough strategy, the work that will be attached to launching strategic initiatives,[1] and the resources required. Each of the strategic initiatives should have an A3 or a project plan behind it, with a clear statement of the issue and current conditions so that all questions can be answered during the executive leadership's deselection meetings.

Once the leadership team is acquainted with the *x* matrix layout, the decision-making filter (shown later in this chapter), and the rhythm of this work, it will focus the team on what is most important, provide a way to track initiatives, and determine which new ones to launch. Once the leadership team trusts this method, it can cut down on a lot of arguing.

Because the *x* matrix is information rich, it can be intimidating to look at. Here, we will break it down into sections, spiraling from the center in a clockwise motion, beginning at nine o'clock (Figure 10.2).

FIGURE 10.2 **The Basic X Matrix**

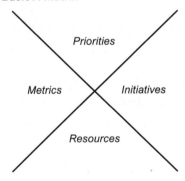

---

1. By "initiative," we mean an activity that requires system resources such as IT, HR, finance, marketing, and so on, to accomplish. An initiative may or may not align with breakthrough strategy; if it does not it should be wait-listed, deselected, or determined to be simply work in progress.

In the center is the basic operating unit of the x matrix: metrics, priorities, initiatives, and resources. In an x matrix for breakthrough strategies, the categories can be renamed True North, breakthrough strategies, initiatives, and resources. We describe each category in the rest of this chapter.

TRUE NORTH

Figure 10.3 focuses on the True North wedge. Begin by listing the organization's True North metrics to the left. These are the critical metrics that help you understand if you are creating and delivering value to the customer. Metrics are generally organized into categories such as quality, cost, delivery, human development and morale, customer satisfaction, and safety.

In creating this x matrix, we seek to understand the interplay between True North and each of the other areas:

- How will the breakthrough strategies help us achieve positive movement on our True North metrics?
- Which of the initiatives most strongly support the breakthrough strategy that is aligned with True North?
- Do the required resources exist to achieve the initiative?

The brand-new breakthrough strategies are usually the most exciting topics of discussion. But we always begin with True North because these are the metrics that guide all of our work.

FIGURE 10.3 True North Wedge

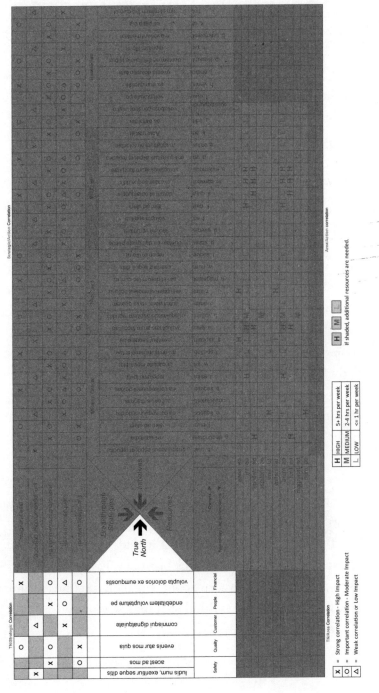

		Strategic/Action Correlation		Area/Action correlation

TN/Strategic Correlation

TN/Area Correlation

X	O	△	O	voluptua dolores ex eumquosits	Financial
	X	O		endebitatem voluptature pe	People
	△	X		comnisqui dignatiqulate	Customer
O	O		X	evenis atur mos quia	Quality
		X	O	acest ad mos	Safety
	X			ludis num, exerfbur seque ditis	

X = Strong correlation - High Impact
O = Important correlation - Moderate Impact
△ = Weak correlation or Low Impact

H	HIGH	5+ hrs per week
M	MEDIUM	2-4 hrs per week
L	LOW	<= 1 hr per week

H	M	

If shaded, additional resources are needed.

175

BREAKTHROUGH STRATEGIES

This chapter assumes that the organization has already undergone a recent strategic development process.[2] At twelve o'clock on the x matrix is the product of that work: the list of high-level strategies that will differentiate the organization in the marketplace. None of these strategies will be incremental improvements. This is the list of must-haves that will carry your organization into the future. The goal is to have three to five breakthrough strategies each year. Figure 10.4 focuses on the breakthrough strategies wedge.

The final line of the breakthrough strategies carries a dose of reality. This is where we list the mission critical must-haves that we call big rocks: huge projects that suck up a lot of resources without necessarily differentiating your organization. A new installation of Epic software, for instance, can cost millions of dollars and thousands of hours in training and other human activities. It is a technological upgrade, but it does not make your organization unique in the marketplace. We can also argue that a new hospital is similar: expensive and time consuming without leaping into the future.

Breakthrough strategies and big rocks alike need an A3 or project plan that defines the initiatives, each of which will go through the deselection filter and move to the three o'clock position.

The list of projects then must include—and clearly differentiate—the great leaps and the big rocks. Every project on this list is a priority, just be clear about which ones are breakthrough and which are necessary undertakings. Color-coding may be in order.

---

2. See Jeff Hunter's *Patient-Centered Strategy* (Catalysis, 2018) as a guide to the strategic development process.

FIGURE 10.4 Breakthrough Strategies Wedge

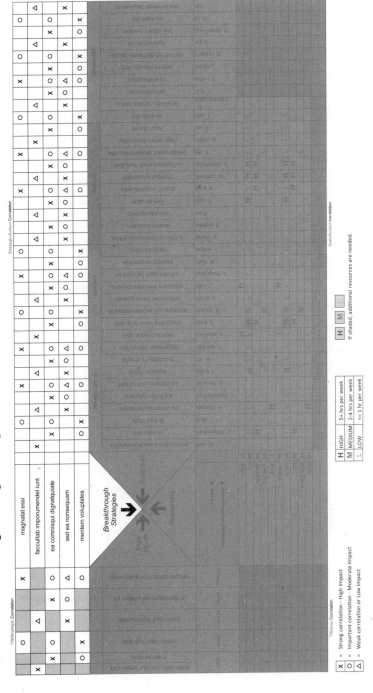

177

Initiatives

The next step is to create a list of initiatives that are necessary to support True North and the breakthrough strategies, then select which of those initiatives gets priority. Figure 10.5 illustrates the initiative categories.Before the team begins this sometimes-contentious work, we create the lens through which we will view each initiative.

A decision filter is one of the best time-saving, aggravation avoidance tools we can offer. Leaders who care will always argue passionately for the initiatives that, from their point of view, matter most. The decision filter is a path to settle arguments for the greater good.

Creating a decision filter for initiatives first requires that everyone on the team agrees on the meaning of each category. What is mission critical? What is important? Definitions must be shared. We propose these definitions but encourage every team to rewrite the words for themselves:

- **Mission critical.** Most deserving of our precious resources at this time. The results will have high impact on both True North and the chosen breakthrough strategies. These are time critical.
- **Important.** Will pursue now but with less emphasis than those deemed mission critical.
- **Wait list.** Will focus on these as soon as resources are freed up from previous categories.
- **Deselected.** We do not have enough information to decide, or the project falls outside the current scope.

FIGURE 10.5 Initiative Categories

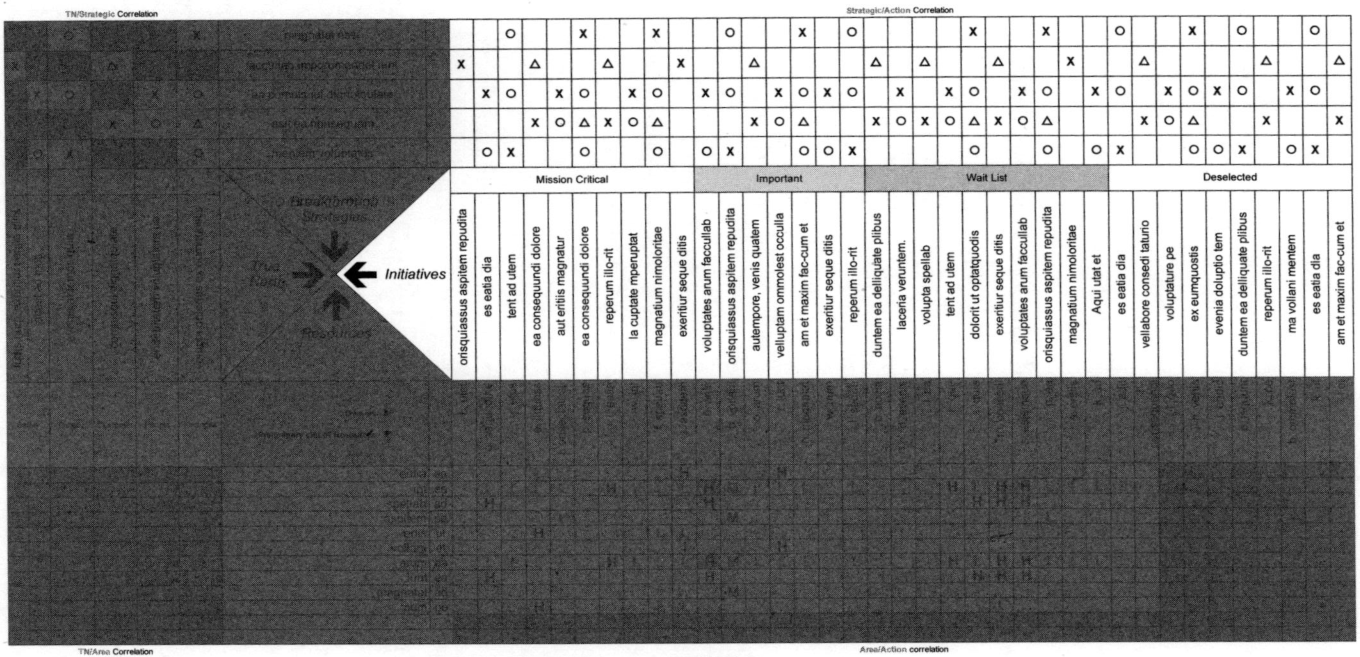

Initiatives

Mission Critical
- onsquassus aspiten repudita
- es eaba dia
- tent ad utem
- ea consequundi dolore
- aut entiis magnatur
- ea consequundi dolore
- reperun illo-nt
- la cupatte mpatpat
- magnatium nimoloritae
- exerfur seque ditis

Important
- voluptates arum faccullab
- onsquassus aspiten repudita
- autempore, venis quatem
- velluptasi ormonst occulla
- am et maxim fac-cum et
- exerfur seque ditis
- reperun illo-nt

Wait List
- durnam ea delliguate pilbus
- lacera verunum
- volupta spellab
- tent ad utem
- dolorit ut optatquodis
- exerfur seque ditis
- voluptates arum faccullab
- onsquassus aspiten repudita
- magnatium nimoloritae
- Aqui utat inbul

Deselected
- es eaba dia
- vellabore consed laturio
- voluptature pe
- ex eumquosts
- evenia doluptio tem
- durnam ea delliguate pilbus
- reperun illo-nt
- ma voliani mentem
- es eaba dia
- am et maxim fac-cum et

Decision Filter

Next, create a series of simple yes-or-no questions. The answers to these questions will lead the team to place each initiative into its proper category. Questions include:

- Do we have enough information to know its impact on True North?
- Is this strongly aligned with our True North metrics?
- Is this part of a breakthrough strategy?
- Is this an operational versus a strategic initiative?
- Is this a statutory, regulatory, or safety requirement?
- Does this initiative benefit the entire system, or is it intended for a single entity or service?
- Is this time sensitive? Do we need to start now to meet a mandated deadline?

In the example shown in Figure 10.6, you can see how each answer leads the team toward one of the four priority categories. This initiative filter is also iterative. If you find that the one you created still leaves you with 25 mission-critical initiatives, it is time to revisit and rewrite the filter. Once the filter is working for you, it is time to select the mission-critical initiatives.

At three o'clock in the x matrix is where the executive team earns its pay. This is where breakthrough strategies and big rocks are broken down into the component initiatives that will make them work. The executive team will then assess each initiative for its importance to the organization's mission and divide them into three or four categories: mission critical, important, wait list, and deselected.

Mission critical includes the 5 to 10 initiatives that cannot wait. This is the work that should begin immediately. If the team believes it has 20 initiatives that cannot wait—and

FIGURE 10.6 **Initiative Filter**

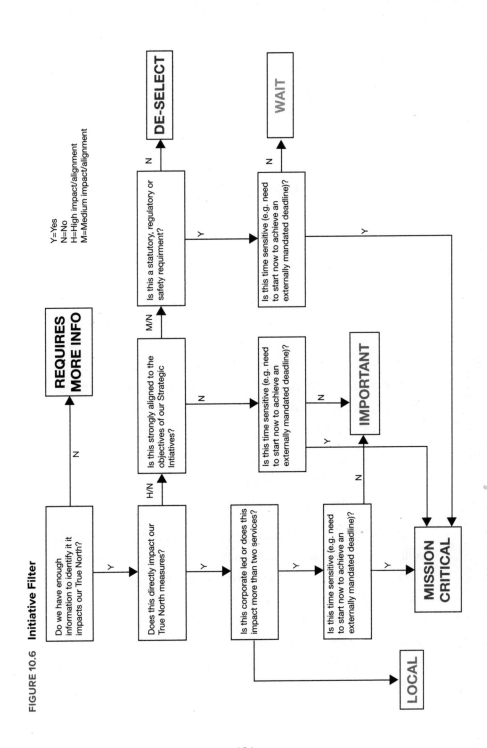

Y=Yes
N=No
H=High impact/alignment
M=Medium impact/alignment

this is where most executive teams get tripped up—it is time to identify the total resources that each initiative requires, list them below, and use the deselection filter. Knowing the limits of your resources will assist you in deselecting initiatives from the mission-critical list.

RESOURCES

For instance, each initiative will require some hours every week from the PI team, from IT, from organizational development for training, and from maintenance and facilities. Will physicians and nurses be on teams to plan or execute the initiative? How about oversight from the lead executive in that area? Figure 10.7 focuses on the resources wedge.

List the resources required, by function, for all projects on the *x* matrix. To the right of that list, note the time required, per week, for each of those functions. Resources required can be color-coded, such as:

- Red: 5 or more hours per week
- Blue: 2 to 4 hours per week
- Green: less than 2 hours per week

Additionally, we encourage people to use fill-in colors to indicate if those resources are available. If a nurse-midwife was needed on a project for at least three hours a week, for instance, but a staffing fluctuation meant that none were available, there would be a blue dot in a pink square in the "nursing" resource category for that project. This is important information as the project is considered for mission-critical status or put off for a time.

FIGURE 10.7 Resources Wedge

FIGURE 10.7 Resources Wedge

TN/Strategic Correlation

Strategic/Action Correlation

Area/Action correlation

TN/Area Correlation

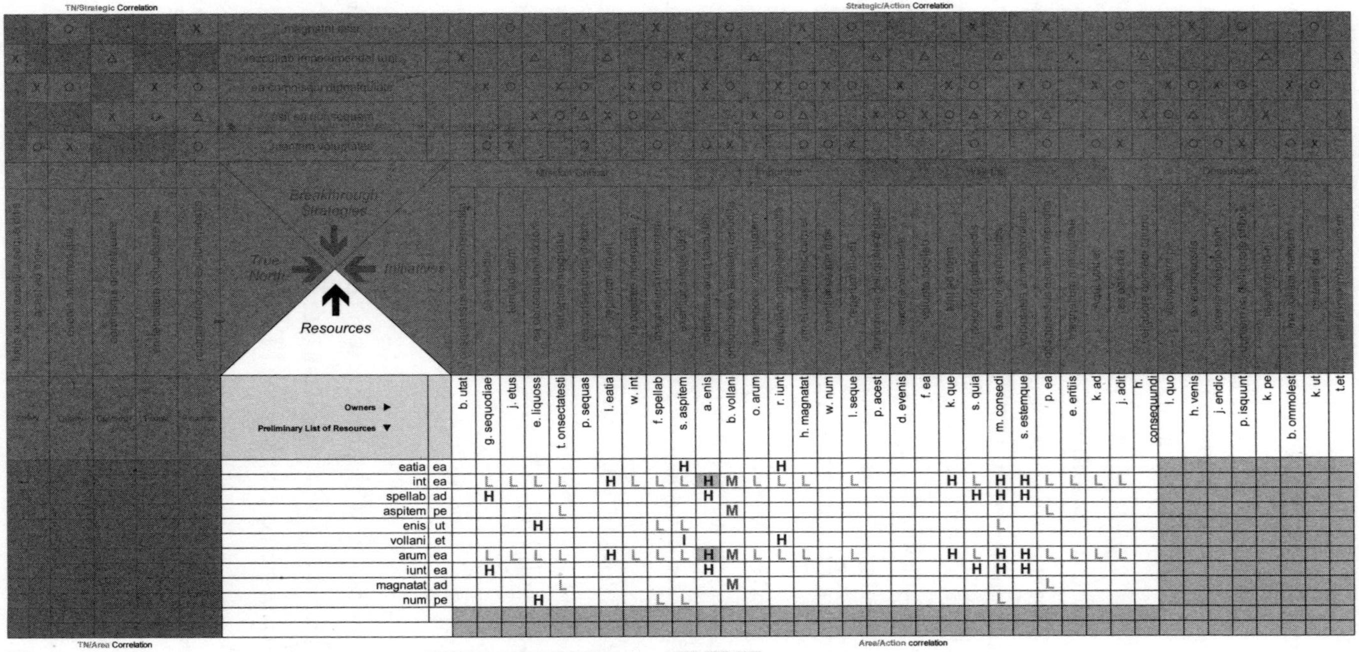

X = Strong correlation - High Impact
O = Important correlation - Moderate Impact
△ = Weak correlation or Low Impact

H	HIGH	5+ hrs per week
M	MEDIUM	2-4 hrs per week
L	LOW	<= 1 hr per week

If shaded, additional resources are needed.

Resources

Owners ▲
Preliminary List of Resources ▲

Breakthrough Strategies

True North

Initiatives

Part of the regularly scheduled work of the executive team, going forward, will be to revisit the list to update work completed in the mission critical category, review what resources are available, and move projects off the waiting list and into mission critical or important, using the selection filter.

Creating a process that executives use to hold each other responsible to accomplish what is on the x matrix is another critical part of this process. If the x matrix languishes in a computer folder and only gets pulled out once a year, all of this will have been a waste of time.

Responsibility can be created, for instance, when each executive creates a list of standard questions to ask of subordinates throughout the management ranks. Some examples include:

- What are your top three priorities?
- Where does this fall on the x matrix?
- What are you going to do next, after this is completed?

When questions that are directly related to the x matrix are part of an executive's standard work with subordinates, the answers will help drive regular updates of the mission-critical projects.

Categories such as wait list and deselected can also provide the time to bring initiatives to greater maturity. Remember that every initiative will most likely have an active problem-solving A3 behind it. Some big rocks like Epic may have project plans that have been created by the IT team, but most other initiatives will require a regular study-and-adjust phase that is best supported by an A3. If a wait-listed initiative does not have an A3, use the time this initiative spends in waiting to create an A3. Digging deeper into the needs of the initiative will only help the executive team in its evaluation.

PART III

Opportunities

Reinvention

The quality revolution is, of course, not the only brink that healthcare stands upon. Massive changes in population and resource distribution are also at the horizon. And the next global pandemic is, perhaps, just now stirring to life inside a bat cave in a little-known region of the world.

We do not know what is coming at us next, but we know that we must not let this massive disruption go to waste.

For many years, we in the medical field have acknowledged major problems and inequities in how healthcare is practiced. We have a system that requires 90-year-old heart patients to drive through snow for follow-up appointments because the clinic is paid by the visit. And health systems lost massive amounts of money during the pandemic, forcing them to lay off nurses, technicians, and physicians, because they could not perform elective surgeries and that's how they get paid—by the procedure.

More recently, we saw that the fee-for-service model did not reward health systems for being prepared for a pandemic, and so most were not ready. The system was not set up to take care of the population as a whole, and so the whole was not cared for.

There were cases of outstanding response by health systems around the country. We saw hospitals with preexisting daily management systems use daily huddles to solve fast-looming problems. The work was inspiring. But it amounted to islands of excellence.

So, we are reevaluating the systems that failed us during the Covid-19 crisis, including supply chains, management processes, care delivery models, and payment systems. Does it make sense to have states and the federal government competing for scarce resources like personal protective equipment? Should all decisions be funneled through a preexisting chain of command? Is it necessary to have infectious patients report to hospitals and testing centers? Do we even need clinics if we can hand out biometric-collecting wrist straps that tell physicians all they need to know while looking at a patient on a screen? How deeply we address these issues will indicate, to some degree, how prepared we can be to meet the next crisis, whether global virus or regional disaster.

For this chapter, therefore, we will set aside incremental improvements in order to address innovation. Many of our assumptions about how to run a healthcare business are still based on a simple transactional concept. Hospital compensation has been based on "heads in beds" for more than 100 years. But we believe that the move to population health, already underway in some areas despite anemic interest from most traditional insurers, is both necessary and inevitable.

Health systems should be paid to keep people healthy and out of hospitals. If that's the case, what will a health system look like? What will it look like to keep a whole population healthy, and how will we match resources to needs?

THE FOURTH VALUE STREAM

In order to prepare for fundamental change, healthcare organizations need to put energy and resources into the fourth value stream: development. This value stream encompasses the creation of new patient experiences. This is not incremental improvement. Here, we leave the traditional methods of care delivery in order to build new models to deliver better value to patients and new processes that can radically change patient outcomes.

Healthcare has spent the past decade or two focused on the first three major value streams: delivery, demand generation, and support. Leaders were not wrong to pursue changes in those areas first. We absolutely needed to change how we delivered care and supported operations.

Now, the time has come to include the development value stream in our work, to create the infrastructure that will foster creative responses to future needs. Technology, pharmaceutical, and manufacturing industries have led the way here, investing serious resources every year in research and development, creating new products and services at breakneck speed to stay competitive. Workers in these industries have been encouraged to take risks and topple the status quo.

The opposite has been true in healthcare delivery. While we have had major breakthroughs in surgical techniques and drug treatments, the actual process of delivering and receiving care has not changed much since World War II. Patients still go to hospitals and clinics, or wait on hold on the telephone, in hopes of accessing most of what they need.

In other industries, development work is referred to as *innovation*, but this is an overused term and too elastic for our purposes. Every way you turn, there are innovation conferences, innovation centers, books, podcasts, and gurus claiming to have the key to using innovation as creative disruption. When innovation experts arrive in healthcare organizations, however, they are usually stifled by the bureaucracy and do little more than erect a fancy idea board, focus on digital apps, or create an incubator for start-ups that may or may not have anything to do with the mission and future of the health system.

What we are talking about is a specific, repeatable process to create or amplify work in the development value stream. This is where teams engage in a fundamental rethinking of the business of delivering healthcare and produce results to be implemented. This process, which we are calling New Care Model Development, is best supported by a principle-driven health system. The bedrock principles here are creating customer value and seeking perfection. The team, and the larger organization, must value the personal traits of curiosity and perseverance to succeed.

Not just any skunk works will do. Simply finding the right geniuses, putting them together in a room, and giving them free rein will only produce ideas that work in that room. Some people claim that, in a lean environment, the best new strategies will be generated at the front line, in the course of the work. We disagree.

We believe that a robust development value stream needs to be separate from the daily work of healthcare. It should be focused on the vision of creating care models that continually improve upon patient experience, quality, and cost of care and led by a dedicated, multidisciplinary team of clinicians, operations specialists, engineers, and support staff—all of whom stand out for being willing to experiment in radical ways. This does not have to be a big team. We have seen effective teams of two people working with an outside coach, at the initial stage. What's critical is that these people practice principle-driven behaviors and that they are allergic to maintaining the status quo or slightly improving on existing ideas.

These personalities can run against the grain of many people in healthcare. Caregivers were not rewarded in medical school for thinking in new ways. We were trained to revere our teachers, to follow best practices and recent research, to find incremental improvements. When looking for clinicians to populate a team of radical innovators, you will be looking for a risk-taker with good interpersonal skills who practices principle-driven behaviors. Deep listening skills are needed for this work.

Our efforts here are still new, but we have seen encouraging results. Before we describe the New Care Model Development process and its early results, we should be clear about the kind of work we are talking about here. This is not a slingshot for every rock.

Think of all the problems you and your organization encounter, and you can visualize all those problems falling into one of four buckets: simple, complicated, complex, and chaotic.[1]

- *Simple problems* have a root cause that is easily identifiable and usually have just one good solution.
- *Complicated problems* have a root cause—sometimes more than one—and have multiple good solutions. Think about addressing the issue of wrong-site surgery,

---

1. With thanks to Dave Snowden and his Cynefin framework. For more information: www.cognitive-edge.com.

for instance. A team will need to include some technical expertise to address a complicated problem, but repeatable solutions that work every time are still possible in this category.

- A *complex problem* has multiple variables with no predictable cause-and-effect relationship. This is where we use small-scale probing, prototyping, and experimentation to allow unique solutions to emerge from the system. Think of a complex problem such as moving a health system's economy from fee-for-service to population health. If a team pondered all of the unknowables while searching for root cause before taking action, it would not be presenting solutions in this decade or, maybe, ever. If a team implemented sweeping changes all at once, on the other hand, it would introduce enormous risk for total system failure. So, teams are encouraged to nail a small boat together, so to speak, and see if it floats.

- The final problem type, *chaotic*, has many roots and courses of action and is usually fast moving. It is unpredictable. Think about a tsunami heading for a nuclear power plant, or a new coronavirus sweeping across the globe unchecked by immune resistance, and you have a chaos problem.

Health systems using lean thinking or Toyota Production System methods have often turned to 3P—production preparation process—to unleash creative solutions. And there is much to applaud in that model. While we were at ThedaCare, teams used these ideas and tools to completely remake the patient care path on hospital units into something we called Collaborative Care. It was breakthrough work that John highlighted in his first book, *On the Mend.* And Seattle Children's mastered 3P while recreating the flow of outpatient surgery in its Bellevue Clinic.[2]

Some work, however, involves deeper questions than how to better coordinate and streamline patient care within a current environment. For complex problems we need to question every assumption about our current state. This is the work we will investigate here.

NEW CARE MODEL DEVELOPMENT

New Care Model Development is a multistep, team-based exploration into a complex problem and its possible solutions. Care models, specifically, are systems designed within regulatory boundaries that deliver value to a population, group, or patient cohort. Successful care models must also provide a good place to work for providers and staff and deliver sustainable business results. They are designed through the coordination of six elements: people, processes, equipment, locations, methods, and information.

New Care Model Development is time-intensive at the opening stage, often referred to as *research* or *discovery.* This is where the team needs to throw out everything they think they know and go out in search of answers to critical questions. What are the patient needs? What are the clinical requirements? What are the payment contracts? What is the current journey? What are competitors doing? What is the current state, really?

---

2. See *Management on the Mend* (ThedaCare Center for Healthcare Value, 2015), pages 42–47.

In this *research* phase, we value divergent thinking. We want the team to remain open to all possibilities. So we broaden the questions even more. What is happening on planet Earth? What are the political, economic, social, technological, and environmental factors that influence our organization and our patients, now or in future? What legal developments are changing the landscape? The team's attention should be open to all factors.

Diversity of experience among team members and respectful communication are requirements here. Team members will be conducting deep interviews with stakeholders, compiling results, and diving down some pretty deep research rabbit holes in order to do the job. Frank and freewheeling discussions inside the team are expected but are only useful if they are respectful and driven by new facts unearthed in diligent investigations.

So far, given the complex nature of care models, three months has been a manageable lower limit for this initial phase. Beware of strict deadlines, however. The team needs breathing space in order to let their minds depart from today. After all, we are looking for ways to win in a radically new way.

This leads to the phase in which the team develops solution *concepts* based on what they learned in their exploratory research, pulling together ideas for radical leaps into the future. After the push to diversify knowledge and thinking, this is the phase where the team converges on a compelling vision for the future. (The team should expect to diverge and converge thinking in just about every phase.)

Developing concepts will often overlap with the *prototype* phase, where ideas are given physical form. Perfection is the enemy of bold experimentation here, and teams are encouraged to fail fast, fail cheap before investing large swaths of resources. This is where a team gets basic proof-of-concept for whether their vision of the future care model is desirable, technically feasible, financially viable, and has the clinical impact they envision. We have used ideas and tools from Design Thinking, agile, and Lean Startup[3]—all popular in the technology sector—to encourage people to sprint toward real working prototypes.

This is the only place, we believe, in a continuous improvement environment where people are encouraged to jump to solutions. That does not mean we want bosses blurting answers. But we do want people thinking about and pursuing workable concepts throughout this process.

Once a team has proven their concepts through prototyping, members must build and *test* the care model, run it in a clinical environment, and evolve based on real needs and limitations. The team—which has also evolved by this point to include new members with new specialties—remains actively involved, collecting and analyzing data to gauge whether the new care model is meeting its targets.

At the end of building and testing the care model it should be *evaluated for scaling.* Go-to-market concepts should be incorporated into the enterprise strategic plan to engage broader operational planning and resources for the diffusion of the new model across the enterprise or new market.

The following case studies illustrate how the process works. These are not included to convince anyone that this is the one right way to accomplish innovation. Our work is too new for that kind of certitude. But we hope there is inspiration.

Seeking Innovation in Eldercare: Care in Place

Atrius Health—the Massachusetts multispecialty group profiled in Chapter 6—was already in a good position to reimagine

---

3. Eric Ries, *The Lean Startup* (Crown Business: 2011).

care delivery when it formally launched an innovation initiative in 2015. About 50 percent of its population was operating under value-based payment contracts, so caregivers and staff were already thinking beyond fee-for-service models. And their team project—focused on creating a new care model for chronically ill, high-risk elderly patients—was led by a popular geriatrician who was motivated for change.

Eliza (Pippa) Shulman, DO, MPH, had seen the too-often disjointed nature of elder care for her entire career. A patient with multiple issues usually has multiple caregivers who are not always perfectly coordinated. A trip to the hospital can exacerbate the disconnect and lead to poor care transitions, loss of functional status, and risk of injury or insult from the hospitalization itself.

As team members discussed different approaches for their work, they quickly focused on the high level of hospital admissions for the fragile elderly that occur on nights and weekends—outside of regular office hours for a person's primary doctor. Confusion and fear were too often part of the patient experience, as well as being a large portion of the total medical expense shouldered by organizations like Atrius Health.

At the advice of a consultant, Adam Ward, Atrius Health leaders staffed a small team to begin researching, including George Higgins and John's son, Ted Toussaint. We watched the experiment with interest from the sidelines.

The first 4 months of this 18-month project were spent mostly in research and investigation. George and Ted found chronically ill patients recently hospitalized for crisis intervention and recorded extensive interviews that they called ethnographies. In one interview, an elderly patient flatly stated, "I would rather die than go to the hospital."

That statement became a fire lit under the team, driving them to push for ways they could get care to people outside of the hospital environment.

While leaders had been focused for many years on reducing 30-day readmissions in this population, initial research led them to think differently about the problem. Instead of reducing readmissions, they asked, "How can we prevent hospital admissions in the first place?"

Of course, this question was only appropriate for some patients. Emergencies like organ failure and sudden physical trauma require hospital-level care. But what about chronically ill patients—someone with congestive heart failure, for instance— who has an emerging crisis at 4 p.m. on a Friday and calls the doctor for advice? These people were almost always advised to go to a hospital.

Working with clinical staff, the team created questions for patients who called with troubling symptoms to determine if the patient needed face-to-face diagnosis and treatment that day. If patients were unable to come into the office, in the existing system, they would have been sent to an ED. Instead, the team envisioned a home-based urgent care service, where a nurse practitioner got in a car and went to the patient to see if that dreaded trip to the ED could be prevented.

This prototype was chosen by the team as the idea with the biggest potential impact, with simple implementation and minimal risk. At the end of their 15-week test in a single region, 37 patients had received a home-based urgent care visit, and 13 of those patients had avoided a trip to the ED—an improvement of about 35 percent. The new care model was dubbed Care in Place.

The results were enough to expand upon the idea and, in the implementation phase, Atrius Health spread Care in Place to 20 clinics in the first year. The team selected clinics based on which ones had more patients potentially in need of this new care model and then met with site leaders to communicate and train people on the needed changes for implementation. However, it quickly became clear that the existing Atrius Health clinic operations did not have enough staff to send nurse practitioners out at a moment's notice. So, they created a partnership with the VNA Care Network in eastern Massachusetts, a visiting nurses' association.

The nurses' association was reluctant to try the new process at first, since it was outside of their standard operating procedures. But the team offered evidence from the Care in Place prototype, and the agency agreed to give it a try with the first 60 patients as a test. The test was successful, and Atrius expanded Care in Place to all of its remaining clinics.

In the first three years of this program, Atrius Health saw a 42 percent reduction in ED use for those who received the Care in Place service, and leaders estimated that it actually halved subsequent hospital admissions in that population. In 2017 and 2018, leaders estimated this saved $2.15 million in unnecessary hospital care. The Care in Place model continues to grow and evolve, and in 2019, leaders were planning to expand its operational hours by leveraging the expertise of paramedics affiliated with Atrius Health clinicians.

By the time Care in Place was scaled up and transitioned into operations, the Atrius Health Center for Innovation had expanded to two teams capable of tackling more than one big question at a time. As the team grew and people pushed for bigger ideas outside of their comfort zones, leadership principles and behaviors like humility, curiosity, and respect became even more important.

"Leader behaviors rooted in principles mitigate a number of ways that projects and teams can fail," Ted says. "People need to feel safe before they can be motivated to push past what is considered possible today."

Staying Out of a Hospital: Medically Home

Leaders and team members in the Center for Innovation deliberated on a next project to pursue. Still enthusiastic about preventing the pain patients can experience from going to the hospital, and in coordination with senior leaders, they decided to expand upon their original work and focus on home hospitalization.

The idea of creating functional hospitals inside patient homes was not new. But, as far as the team could discover, nobody had yet made it work sustainably. So, they were happy to meet a small start-up company called Medically Home that had experience experimenting with the model and was looking for an established health system to partner with on development.

Following a similar new care model development process over a multiyear period, and this time with an expanded team including the founders of Medically Home, the innovation team researched, prototyped, and piloted a new, fully scalable home-hospital care model.

The new model, also called Medically Home, combined technology and clinical expertise to provide hospital-level care in patients' homes, including medications, meals, home health aides, and all other services provided by traditional hospitals. Caregivers staffed a medical command center 24/7 at Atrius Health while high-tech equipment and supplies were deployed to patients' homes. Acute rapid response was available 24 hours per day.

Patients were referred to the program from ambulatory clinics, urgent care centers, or selected emergency departments. As a first step, all patients underwent clinical and social eligibility screening to see if their needs could be met outside a hospital. If patients cleared the screening, they were offered the option of hospitalization at home.

A clinician and a technician then set up equipment such as biometric monitoring and communications, completed a medication reconciliation, and assessed the patient in conjunction with a physician back at the medical command center. The care team included physicians, nurse practitioners, skilled nurses, therapists, and others, providing care that included intravenous therapy, remote vitals monitoring, basic diagnostics, a dedicated phone line, and a video communication setup.

Physicians, nurse practitioners, and nurses located in the medical command center would virtually round on patients, monitor vitals, and document routine and status changes in real time. Various caregivers also visited the patient at home to provide imaging services, meals, and personal care.

Patient feedback on the new model has been positive. The pilot conducted with 68 patients received perfect scores in both willingness to recommend the program and communication with doctors and nurses. As one patient expressed, "Every stage of this whole experience, everyone came and helped whenever I needed, for whatever I needed. I never felt alone in this."

As of fall 2019, Medically Home had successfully completed over 100 in-home inpatient episodes. Episodes were, on average, 30 days in length from admission to discharge and involved two phases of care: acute and restorative. Patients in the acute phase are equivalent to hospital inpatients, receiving all the services outlined above. Patients in the restorative phase are those who would have been discharged to home or a skilled nursing facility. The focus during restorative phase shifts to prevention of further exacerbation, advance care planning, teaching, and addressing the social determinants of health such as transportation, food security, and the like. Patients receive comprehensive, patient-centered services tailored to their needs at an average savings of 15 to 30 percent when compared to equivalent hospital-based care.

So far, quality and safety outcomes have been equivalent or better than traditional hospital care. The pilot population had an overall 30-day readmission rate of 8.1 percent versus 22 percent in an equivalent population with normal hospital care. (Patients treated for acute exacerbation of heart failure had a 6 percent readmission rate.) While careful clinical screening seeks to ensure that patients are appropriate for this care model, 7.4 percent of patients needed to be escalated to a higher level of care, such as a hospital ICU.

Many patients served by this program were multimorbid and met criteria for palliative or hospice care. All patients had advance care planning and almost 20 percent were discharged to palliative or hospice services.

A key breakthrough in Medically Home was a scalable economic model enabled through creative staffing, centralization of physician resources, and new technology. The team estimates that this home-hospital model can replace 20 to 30 percent of all inpatient hospital stays, and it is designed to be financially viable at a national scale. While the original pilot was launched in Massachusetts, Medically Home has begun expanding to other parts of the United States including the Midwest and Pacific Northwest.

If scaled to its full potential, Medically Home could make a substantial contribution to the current crisis of national healthcare spending.

FIVE FIRST STEPS

Building a New Care Model Development process requires some new thinking as well as new infrastructure. Ideas that underpin this work have been pulled from agile, Design Thinking, and lean product and process development, as well as from organizational excellence, so leaders must be prepared to incorporate new concepts. And since this work is about the strategic direction of the organization, the senior executive team will need to be front and center.

For instance, consider secrecy. Usually, we are proponents of transparency in healthcare operations. But this work actually requires protection from prying eyes. For this team to feel safe to play with wild ideas, rumor mills must be avoided. The last thing people on the front line need are speculative whispers going around about the closing of a hospital.

Also, a New Care Model Development team does not begin the work by studying current conditions in a target area. A clinician or engineer with decades of experience cannot help but bring their knowledge of processes into the room. And we value their expertise. But we are not studying current processes and inviting frontline opinions here. We are trying to imagine and create new cloth. So, we need to lay the groundwork.

What follows are the five initial steps an organization needs to take to prepare for a New Care Model Development team.

Create a Team

Selection criteria for this team must favor traits and behaviors over professional accomplishments. Team members should display humility and curiosity above all else. Also, they should be known for having an entrepreneurial spirit—the kind of people who are happy to try out new ideas or different methods and want to rope others into their efforts.

Youth can be an advantage, as well. A certain amount of neuroplasticity, at any rate, is required to imagine a world and human interactions that are beyond what is known.

The core team does not need to be large, but it should be dedicated to this work. There can also be half-time people on this team, or people with functional knowledge of IT, EHR,[4] or finance who come in to consult. But the core team should be completely invested.

The leader will be a kind of chief engineer, with deep knowledge about product (type of care) and customers (patients). This role was filled by Pippa Shulman in the Care in Place example above. In that case, Atrius senior leaders knew they needed to rethink aspects of geriatric care, so they selected a clinical leader who was passionate about the field and dissatisfied with the care her patients received.

Pippa's dissatisfaction with the existing care model was crucial to that team. She was willing to disrupt the status quo, even if it could create conflict with her peers, to help her patients. That is the kind of leader the team requires.

Dedicate Space

Technology companies have embraced the concept of the *obeya*,[5] which was popularized at Toyota Motor Corp. The obeya is often referred to as a war room or a brain. It is a space with enough room for the team to work and to visually capture and display their process and progress. There should be enough wall

---

4. Electronic health records.
5. *Obeya* is Japanese for "big room" or "great room."

space for the team to build the story of their concept and plan, giving them a way to introduce newcomers or functional consultants to the full story.

The space should be secure to avoid cross-contamination. Think of it as a negative pressure room. The outside organization should not be hearing about any early speculation or untested ideas. And the team should be protected from pressure and presumptions from the larger organization.

Plan the Process

As we outlined above, there are five essential steps in the process: research, concept, prototype, test, and evaluate for scale. There are many ways people codify design and development processes, and over time, many organizations develop their own, tailored to their specific culture and needs. Some organizations may have many of the right steps already in place but using different words. In that case, the above list exists as a check to ensure all elements are in play.

These steps are the arc of the work but are not always rigidly followed. Team members should respect the creative process and allow for overlapping of some steps and diversions at any point.

Establish Governance

Oversight of the New Care Model Development team should reside in a small committee that acts as both buffer and yoke between the team and senior executives. Communication is important here because nobody wants to get three months down the line on a concept just to have the CEO say *no*. On the other hand, the team should not be listening to a lot of opinions from senior executives, or anxiously trying to read their facial expressions for approval. Even if senior executives are requesting innovation in specific areas, the governance committee still acts as a buffer.

The governance committee will create clear definitions of what success and failure look like. Those definitions may very well change from one project to the next, but it is important to have clarity here so that the governance committee can devise its own decision filters to guide the work and team.

If there are barriers in the team's way, the governance committee is there to run interference, as well as acting as an extra layer of security, protecting the team and its work from the rest of the organization. Because this team is solving tomorrow's problems—not today's—members of the governance committee may also be chief interpreters of the work.

Provide Funding

The team will need access to resources, of course, and it is useful to think of funding as three buckets.

In the research and discovery phase, the team should feel empowered to make small purchases. Nobody is buying solutions here. But if the team wants to experiment with pieces of technology or offer honorariums to patients in exchange for lengthy interviews, that should be available. This bucket might contain $5,000.

The second bucket is empty until approved by the special governance committee, and this is for costlier items needed to flesh out new care models. For instance, the team might need a nurse practitioner for a month to assist in developing and testing workflows for home visits. An organization should set aside something like $20,000 to $50,000 in anticipation of these expenses.

The third bucket is also a negotiation between the team and its governance committee. After creating a business plan for the new care model and pitching it to the organization, the team will be expected to present a budget to bring the idea to scale. So, the third bucket is like the wallet of a venture capitalist—empty until approval.

The future of healthcare, we believe, rests on the creation of development value streams. Covid-19 exposed major weaknesses and opportunities for us as caregivers. We have been needing new care models for years. But now, the lives of our grandchildren depend on our ability to innovate.

We can push ourselves past immediate fixes, go further than a cool new app. If we can think and act differently, if we can build repeatable process to foster creativity as outlined here, we can get there.

ANOTHER FUTURE

The other new piece of our work going forward is a continuation of this book. We all learn from the stories of others. We have seen this in the network and at every conference and summit where our colleagues across the world tell the stories of what they tried, what failed, and what became something greater than they imagined. True stories help illuminate our own paths.

Changing leadership behaviors is not a one-off project. Learning how to best communicate with others cannot be accomplished in a single workshop. Actually working at these behaviors and becoming better leaders is an ongoing practice that requires regular reflection and communication. Like any regular practice—spiritual, musical, athletic—our understanding of what we are doing deepens and changes over time.

So, we will be including regular updates of some of the stories you have read here, plus new case studies. We intend to roll these updates up into a second edition of this book in 2022.

We are deeply humbled by the work of the people highlighted in this book and the many others we have been so privileged to work with throughout the years. Our job is to continue to facilitate this remarkable community of committed learners as we learn, share, and connect with each other to make the world a better place. Our mission is no less than that. We hope this book can add to our goal to keep the conversation going.

ACKNOWLEDGMENTS

This book has been a big team effort on a journey that has taught us so much. We have been blessed with many who have crossed our paths and changed the course of our mindset. Without the many experiments, teachers, coaches, and mentors from around the world, this body of knowledge would not have been possible. Our role has been to work with and observe many healthcare leaders as they learn the methods of organizational excellence. Leaders have helped us to create clarity by testing hypotheses, practicing new ways of thinking, and helping us learn what leaders need to know to transform organizational culture for improvement. This has occurred in many countries and in very different cultures. We have been humbled by the amazing work of dedicated healthcare leaders as they change themselves. As we have learned from them, we have tested and improved both our thinking and our learning systems with the intent to help others learn the concepts, tools, traits, and behaviors that make up the organizational excellence method. In fact, we have standardized much of the learning content, which we have outlined in this book. Now we and you can continue to learn from and improve it.

As a community, we grow and delight in each other's success and contributions. We would like to expressly thank the myriad of leaders who have contributed to this work. These people and many of you continue to challenge, influence, and inspire us every day. For that we are sincerely grateful.

A special thank you to those who allowed us into their world as this book was written. Your reflection and willingness to share your personal thoughts as well as the work of your organization is so much appreciated. It is the backbone of our book.

Dr. Susan P. Ehrlich, CEO of Zuckerberg San Francisco General Hospital; Dan Schuette, former Board Chair of St. Charles, and Joe Sluka, CEO, St. Charles, Bend Oregon; Megan Haase, a board member, family nurse practitioner, and the CEO of Mosaic Medical of central Oregon. Don Shilton, retired CEO, St. Mary's General Hospital; Christine Henhoeffer, RN, and a past board chair of St. Mary's General Hospital in Kitchener, Ontario. Eric Dickson, MD, CEO of UMass Memorial Health Care in Worcester, Massachusetts. Kathy Krusie, senior vice president, Community Physician Network Operations at Community Health Network. Grey Dube, CEO of Leratong Regional Hospital Johannesburg, South Africa, and Gladys Bogoshi, CEO of Charlotte Maxeke Johannesburg Academic Hospital, Gauteng province, South Africa. Carlos Scholz-Moreno, director of strategic initiatives for a large multispecialty physician group in Northern California; Didier Rabino, lean sensei, Value Capture, and former vice president, HealthEast; Kathryn Correia, CEO, Legacy Health and former CEO, Health East. Georgina Gardner, RN, manager of the pediatrics unit at UMass Memorial; Kathleen Hylka, director of Strategic Space Planning at UMass Memorial. At Berkshire Healthcare NHS Foundation Trust: Julian Emms, chief executive, Rosemary Warne, clinical director, Nikola Pollard, head of financial transformation, and Alex Gild, CFO. At UMass Memorial: Tod Wiesman, chief learning officer and VP of organizational people development, Laura Flynn, director of performance, learning, and education, Jena Adams, a consultant in organizational and people development. Sandra Geiger, SVP of People at Atrius Health; Robert Azevedo, MD, physician in chief of a large multispecialty physician group in Northern California; Al Pilong Jr, former COO, Munson Healthcare and CEO of Novant Health UVA Health System; Eliza (Pippa) Shulman, DO, MPH, Atrius. The innovators, teachers, and coaches of the Catalysis faculty: Adam Ward, George Higgins, and Ted Toussaint. And Heidi Betzinger, leader of the Catalysis Development Value Stream.

We were also supported and influenced by so many others.

We are grateful to Margie Hagene, Catalysis faculty. Her work with personal A3 and coaching is groundbreaking, and without her clear vision, great communication, and dedication we would not have been able to connect traits and behaviors of leaders as a gap in the transformation journey.

A special thank you to Karl Hoover, Catalysis faculty and wonderful coach who developed the idea of using radar chart assessments for personal improvement.

Thank you to our Catalysis board of directors: Kathryn Correia, Orry Fiume, Mark Hallett, George Koenigsaecker, Kevin McNamara, John Shook, Steve Shortell, Kevin Shulman, Ken Snyder, Jeff Thompson, Peter Ward, and Lisa Yerian. Your guidance has helped us thrive and stay true to our vision and mission

Thank you to the Catalysis staff—you are a brilliant team of people. Without you, John and I would be lost and much less effective. We are grateful to you every day. A special thank you to Heidi Betzinger, Angela Brubacher, Nicole Christensen, Karen Flom, Peter Mariahazy, Paul Pejsa, Rachel Regan, Sara Thompson, Stephanie Van Vreede, Brian Veara, Chris Weisbrod, and Sara Woerishofer.

Our appreciation to the Shingo Institute, Utah State University, for the deep work they continue to inspire and develop.

Our work would not be possible without their leadership and model.

We are saddened by the passing of Paul O'Neill, who died the month before this manuscript was completed. He was a Catalysis founding board member and truly the world's greatest safety leader. He embodied every behavior we have written about and inspired us all.

Our roots lie with LEI: John Shook, James Womack, Jean Cunningham, and Josh Howell—thank you for jointly publishing this piece of work. We were born from the LEI model and continue to be inspired by your work. We value our relationship as we share commitment to the lean community.

We share a great sense of gratitude to Emily Adams; without you the community would not hear our message. Thank you so much for demanding clarity while developing a cohesive message and helping us to author a collection of learning.

Thank you to Helen Zak; we still feel your voice and mission as we work through how to present new thinking to the community. As the leader who began the forums model—thank you for creating a system for learning, sharing, and connecting with executive leaders around the world. This model continues to grow and improve with the support and leadership now provided by Rachel Regan, Kathy Franklin, Elizabeth Warner, Pam Helander, and Elaine Meade.

The foundation of our work often lies with all of our Catalysis Healthcare Value Network members past and present. Thank you for the commitment to learning, experimenting, and sharing that has built a community of operational excellence. Your voices resonate as we ask you to share your experiences and influence each other.

We have learned so much from all the leaders in our CEO forums, US and European. As they share their development and experiment with their learning in the work, we can bring forward guiding examples for others to try. This book is full of the evidence they have provided.

We continue to be committed to our work in South Africa. A special thank you to Norman Faull and Anton Grutter from Lean Institute Africa for bringing us into their work. Together we are making a difference in a part of the world that has few resources but great passion and heart for improvement.

Much of our work is focused on the executive and board leadership. Without our valued partners, Value Capture and KPMP Canada/UK, to extend our reach and focus on the ground, we would not be successful. Our partnerships have made us all stronger and extended our reach around the world. Jake Raymer, founder of IEX, we are so grateful for the relationship we have developed over the last years. Your insight is most evident as we discuss strategy deployment and the x matrix. Theresa Moore, you advanced our thinking and standardization in so many ways! We appreciate your partnership.

Our work continues because of our faculty. This group of dedicated practitioners, leaders, teachers, and coaches continues to be the backbone of who we are. You share our vision and spread our mission though the transformation process and bring with it additional insight that helps us all continue to improve. A sincere thank you to Katie Anderson, Joanne Bicknell, Lydia Chudleigh, Yvonne DeGroot, Mike De Luca, Jennifer Dieter, Patsy Engel, Mark Graban, Nancy Gurnee, Michael Hoseus, Jeff Hunter, Tim Johnson, Jim Marks, MD, Jill Menzel, Mike Orzen, Steve Player, Mike Radtke, Maryjeanne Schaffmeyer, Jason Schulist, Don Shilton, Scott Smith, Ted Toussaint, Adam Ward, Didier Rabino, Mark Hamel, and Linda Mirkes.

Our gratitude continues for all our teachers, mentors, and coaches. Thank you for continuing to share your insight, support, and gifts with us. Without Jose Bustillo and George Koenigsaecker, we may not have found the path that our journey is now grounded in.

Tom Hartman joined us to develop our executive coaching. His deep knowledge of lean, executive roles, and coaching made us better. As we worked together we are so grateful to him for making the standards explicit. He helped us to standardize our coaching approach based on the Shingo principles. He also helped us apply the principles to improve our lean management system training.

Our families are always the greatest source of support and inspiration. In fact, they are the team that keeps us going. They see us for who we are and challenge our thinking in different ways. Without them the grounding in our work would suffer. We cannot express the gratitude we feel for their unconditional love and dedication that gives is the courage to continue this work. To our true partners in life, John's wife, Susan Toussaint, and my husband, John Utrie, we say *thank you!*

APPENDIX

The images provided here allow you to more easily reproduce them as standalone documents as you incorporate them in your journey.

FIGURE 1.1 **Shingo Principles**

FIGURE 2.1 **Board Assessment Questionnaire**

This questionnaire can be used to rate an organization's progress in using improvement processes. Rate statements 1 through 17 on a scale of 1–4 as follows:

1. **Not started.** No continuous improvement program.

2. **Beginning.** Planning has begun, activities may have started, but no significant engagement and no significant progress.

3. **Growing.** Teaching, engaging, succeeding, struggling, and failing are all occurring as the teams make slow, steady, and sometimes painful progress forward. Leaders, physicians, and associates alike are becoming progressively more involved, more committed, and more capable of learning from both successes and failures.

4. **Sustaining.** The organization's principle-driven lean behaviors can be described as teaching, mentoring, supporting, encouraging, enabling, humbling, steady, predictable, teachable, engaged, committed, and disciplined. Cultural behaviors drive many successes and also occasional failures with A3 thinking (or an equivalent structured problem-solving method) being applied in all cases.

1. Board members have been trained and participated in three gemba visits per year and have practiced asking open-ended questions. Board members have participated in at least one education session on improvement thinking this year.

2. Board members are offered opportunities to tour best practice improvement organizations. Some members participate every year.

3. The board has clearly defined in writing and practice the role of governance versus management.

4. The board evaluates improvement plans and organizational performance at each board meeting with a set of clear top-level metrics (True North) for quality, safety, cost, patient satisfaction, and staff engagement.

5. The board works with management on a regular basis (at least three times a year) to define and reevaluate the strategic direction of the organization.

6. The board understands and reviews management's A3 presentations at each board meeting.

7. The board exhibits ideal behaviors in the practice of governance as outlined in a written board code of conduct.

8. The board has defined the behavioral expectations for Board members.

9. The board has at least one member that has extensive experience with lean/improvement.

10. The board has a system to assure board member succession planning includes questions regarding potential members' willingness to learn the lean method and practice it at the governance level.

11. There is a process to onboard new members to the organization's improvement methodology.

12. The board has developed an internal CEO succession plan that includes identifying potential successors, regular updates on their progress and experiences, and a focus on the behavioral traits that would allow the person to be an effective lean CEO.

13. At a minimum of once a year, the board reviews the organization's commitment to lean methods, outcomes of lean management, and leader development across administrative and medical staff.

14. Board members regularly identify areas for improvement in governance practices.

15. At least one committee is practicing some aspect of lean thinking in their governance activities including but not limited to improvement projects identified by board members using PDSA (plan-do-study-act) thinking for problem solving or Pareto analysis of board problems.

16. Some portion of every board meeting is devoted to improving the board's practices.

17. Board performance and improvements are visual, displayed where all can see them.

FIGURE 3.1 **One of Mr. Dube's Earliest Radar Charts That Helped Guide His Behavioral Change**

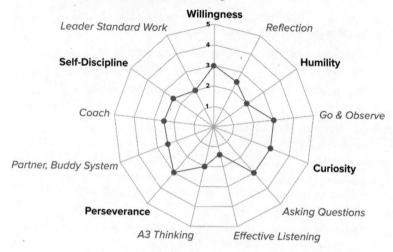

FIGURE 6.1 **A Sample of the Standards of Respect Card Deck**

FIGURE 6.2 Stepping Up Respect: Manager Feedback. These are the questions to be answered by a manager's selected review group.

In the following areas, how should this person change his or her behavior or actions?	Do much less	Do less	Don't change	Do more	Do much more
Acknowledge					
1 Demonstrates gratitude (says thank you; comments positively on others' actions; recognizes good work)	○	○	○	○	○
2 Makes others a priority (shows personal interest in others; makes time for others; makes personal connections)	○	○	○	○	○
3 Honors diversity (is careful not to make assumptions based on appearance, name, gender, race, role, etc.)	○	○	○	○	○
Listen					
4 Gives full attention (stops other activities to focus on the speaker; stops using technology when others are talking)	○	○	○	○	○
5 Clarifies Understanding (summarizes or asks follow-up questions to ensure understanding of intended message)	○	○	○	○	○
6 Displays patience (pauses before responding; lets others finish speaking)	○	○	○	○	○
7 Seeks others' perspectives (asks if everyone was heard; invites others to speak; welcomes everyone's contribution)	○	○	○	○	○
Communicate					
8 Shares generously (provides all relevant and appropriate information; shares knowledge: shares the good, the bad, and the ugly; makes sure hand-offs are clear)	○	○	○	○	○
9 Confirms prior understanding (asks what others need to know before instructing/providing information)	○	○	○	○	○
10 Communicates considerately (uses simple language to aid others' understanding; uses best medium to share information, e.g. in-person, email, phone)	○	○	○	○	○
Be Responsive					
11 Shares updates (keeps people informed of progress; alerts others if deadlines are at risk)	○	○	○	○	○
12 Prioritizes the important (determines what's important and acts on it; is willing to delay less urgent tasks/items)	○	○	○	○	○
13 Delivers results (knows and meets deadlines; follows through on commitments)	○	○	○	○	○
Be a Team Player					
14 Is collaborative (commits to and acts upon shared goals; collaborates and/or cooperates whenever possible; brainstorms for solutions)	○	○	○	○	○
15 Helps others (says "yes" to requests for assistance; says what they can do, not just what they can't; proactively offers to help)	○	○	○	○	○
16 Helps others meet their goals (sets others up for success, e.g., next shift, teammates, other departments, etc.)	○	○	○	○	○
17 Considers others (shows up on time; shows care about how his/her work affects others)	○	○	○	○	○
Be Kind					
18 Displays empathy for others (recognizes and honors others' pain and joy; delivers bad news sensitively; comforts those who need it)	○	○	○	○	○
19 Manages own emotions (shields patients and families from irritation or frustration; displays patience under pressure; gives instructions and/or responds with a calm voice)	○	○	○	○	○
20 Is gracious (shares credit when things go right; takes ownership when things go wrong)	○	○	○	○	○
21 Intervenes for others (steps in when someone else is being treated unfairly or poorly; stands up for those that may need support or reinforcement)	○	○	○	○	○
Open-ended question					
1 What additional feedback, if any, would you provide to this manager?					

FIGURE 6.3 **Stepping Up Respect: Manager Feedback Report**

These are the three items identified across all raters as those you demonstrate well. Congratulation! Keep it going!

The three items you should continue demonstrating:

14	Prioritize the important (determine what's important and acts on it; is willing to delay less important task/items)
9	Shares generously (provides all relevant and appropriate information; shares knowledge; shares the good, the bad and the ugly; makes sure hand-offs are clear)
1	Greets people (is friendly; smiles and says hello; introduces self to others; uses peoples' names)

These are the top three items identified across all raters that are opportunities for improvement.

Your three priority items:

23	Manage owns emotions (shields patients and families from irritation or frustration; displays patience under pressure; gives Instructions and/or responds with a calm voice)
7	Displays patience (pauses before responding; lets others finish speaking)
19	Sets others up for success (next shift, teammates, other departments, etc.)

Source: Special thanks to CEO Eric Dickson for sharing his annual Stepping Up Respect review.

FIGURE 7.1 **Organizational Leadership Self-Assessment Questionnaire**

This questionnaire can be used to rate an organization's leadership. Rate the statements in sections 1 through 6 below on a scale of 1–4 as follows:

1. **Not started.** No continuous improvement program.

2. **Beginning.** Planning has begun, activities may have started, but no significant engagement and no significant progress.

3. **Growing pains.** Teaching, engaging, succeeding, struggling, and failing are all occurring as the teams make slow, steady, and sometimes painful progress forward. Leaders, physicians, and associates alike are becoming progressively more involved, more committed, and more capable of learning from both successes and failures.

4. **Sustaining.** The organization's principle-driven lean behaviors can be described as teaching, mentoring, supporting, encouraging, enabling, humbling, steady, predictable, teachable, engaged, committed, and disciplined. Cultural behaviors drive many successes and also occasional failures with A3 thinking (or an equivalent structured problem-solving method) being applied in all cases.

1. System Top Management Engagement

1.1. The board you primarily work with is supportive of the organizational commitment to lean.

2. Local Organization Top Management Engagement

2.1. Organization leaders are all competent lean leaders, spending at least 40 percent of their time teaching, coaching, and mentoring the organization.

2.2. Organization leaders participate in one improvement activity each week with VPs participating daily as part of their management standard work.

2.3. The organization has a strategy deployment process that connects the breakthrough strategies to the frontline work.

2.4. Lean competence is a requirement for managerial promotion.

2.5. Principles drive behavior to the extent that these principles are clearly observable as cultural traits. Note: these behaviors should be evident in the daily work and service that is provided to the patients.

2.6. Organization leaders fulfill their role as lean leaders by leading some improvement events and participating regularly in improvement activities.

3. Commitment to Improvement

3.1. The organization embraces the pursuit of perfect service, quality, and patient satisfaction, understanding that this will also progressively reduce cost.

3.2. Organizational leadership understands that improvement is essential to the fulfillment of its mission.

3.3. There is no "blame and shame" environment so it is safe to expose problems.

3.4. Patients join with team members in improvement activities to support and accelerate the rate of improvement.

3.5. Continuous improvement is a powerful source of personal satisfaction for providers, caregivers, support staff, and top management.

4. Teamwork

4.1. Cross-functional teams (including providers, caregivers, and support staff) operate naturally and effectively.

4.2. Employees are trained in team building and are encouraged to participate in lean improvement activities.

4.3. All goals are identified as team goals encouraging each team member to engage in both goal development and execution.

4.4. Teams respond well to management coaching and mentoring with significant team initiative and capability being demonstrated.

4.5. Team-driven improvements result in the achievement of team goals with associated sharing of best practices.

(continued)

FIGURE 7.1 **Organizational Leadership Self-Assessment Questionnaire**
continued

5. Respect Every Individual

5.1. The organization is enjoying increased employee morale.

5.2. Senior leaders focus on raising the skill and ability of providers, caregivers, and support staff through formal training and the daily management process.

5.3. Senior leaders show respect for providers, caregivers, and support staff, keeping them safe from harm with accidents and near misses requiring an A3 (or equivalent structured problem-solving method).

5.4. Resources that are no longer required for reacting to problems are redeployed to proactive roles, thereby accelerating improvement.

5.5. Promotions from within the organization demonstrate managerial commitment to the organizational culture, instead of hiring from the outside.

6. New Care Model Development

6.1. Organizational leaders understand and support the need for the development of new care models.

6.2. There is a culture of innovation where leaders have patience for development, teams take appropriate risks, and new services are created regularly.

6.3. Strategy deployment clearly lays out challenging goals around the development of new care models.

6.4. Resources that are outside of operations are dedicated for the purpose of developing new care models.

6.5. A robust and repeatable care model development process that is separate from daily improvement processes continually delivers new care models into operations.

FIGURE 8.1 A3 Personal Improvement.

Personal Improvement A3 Title:

Date:
Authored by:
Coach:

Background
Why should I improve myself in order to be a coach / leader who creates an organization filled with problem solvers? Why this, why now?

Current State
Habits / Actions I Currently Take → Outcomes From My Current Habits / Actions
(Strengths and Limitations)

Opportunity Statement - 1 Concise Sentence

Goals / Targets
New Desired Condition. What does better look like for me? What, How Much, By When?

Analysis
Reasons for My Personal Performance/ for My Current Strong Habits and Limiting (Gap) Habits

Proposed Countermeasures
What experiments will I try on myself to become a better coach / leader of problem solvers?

Plan / Next Steps
What steps will I take and when? What is my practice plan to develop new habits?

Follow Up
How will I know if there's improvement?
How will I know if things are off plan?
How will I make time to practice?
What is my process for ongoing reflection / P-D-C-A?
Who else will I involve?

FIGURE 9.1 **Radar Chart**

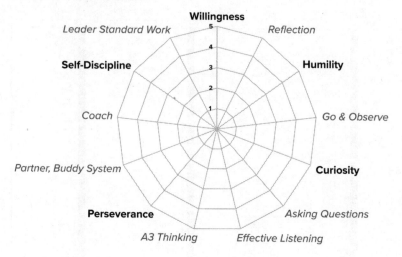

FIGURE 9.2   **Sample Effective Questions**

1. What is the problem you are trying to solve?

2. How would you describe what is happening as opposed to what should be happening?

3. What have you looked at or heard about?

4. What makes you sure you have a cause/effect link?

5. What have you thought of trying?

6. What impact do you expect that countermeasure to have?

7. What make that so important?

8. What might you do to figure out _____ about _____ (patient, customer, vendor etc.)?

9. How do you learn about that?

10. What process do we have to facilitate that discussion with _____?

11. Tell me more about what you mean when you say _____?

12. What would be an exception to that?

13. What is the definition of _____?

14. How do you set that up and present it?

15. What do you know about _____?

16. How do you know we're not doing that?

17. What does good look like today?

18. How do we know what they want?

19. How do you determine demand?

20. How do you know cause and effect?

21. Who have you spoken to about this?

22. What do you know about that?

23. Tell me one thing you think about that.

24. What evidence do you have so far?

25. What impact does that have on _____?

26. What improvements have occurred so far?

(continued)

FIGURE 9.2 **Sample Effective Questions** *continued*

27. Describe the obstacles to _____?

28. What was the outcome?

29. So where does it break down?

30. How could you show that visually in your A3?

31. That sounds like a solution—lets go back to the left side.

32. What have we learned from _____ about navigating that?

33. Who currently owns that process?

34. Who are the stakeholders?

35. How will you explain that to them?

36. What are the other scenarios that might happen if you deliver that message?

37. What factors contribute to this?

38. How was that decision made?

39. How do you know there is variation?

FIGURE 9.3   **Radar Chart with Scores**

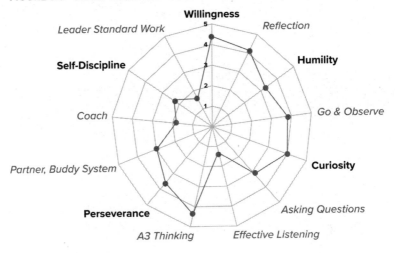

FIGURE 9.4   **Willingness Wedge**

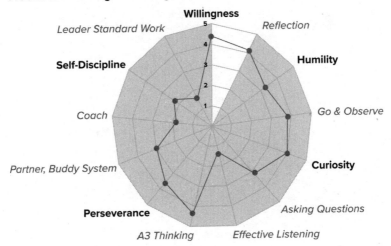

FIGURE 9.5 **Humility Wedge**

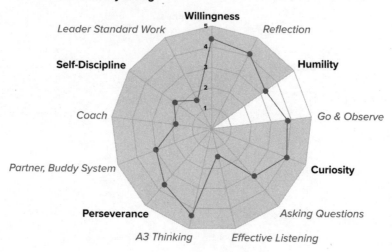

FIGURE 9.6 **Curiosity Wedge**

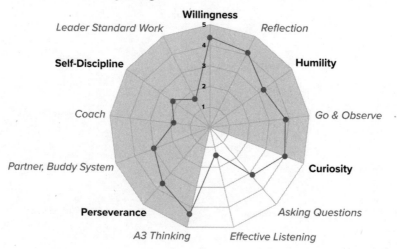

FIGURE 9.7 **Perseverance Wedge**

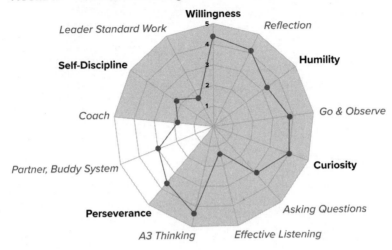

FIGURE 9.8 **Self-Discipline Wedge**

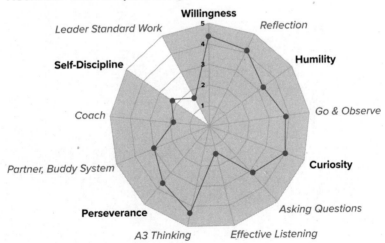

FIGURE 10.1 **X Matrix**

Breakthrough Strategies — Initiatives — Resources — True North

magnatat essi

faccullab imporumendel iunt

ea commisqui dignatquiate

asit ea nonsequam

mentem voluptates

Owners ▲
Preliminary List of Resources ▼

Resources
eatia ea
int ea
spellab ad
aspitem pe
enis ut
vollani et
arum ea
iunti ea
magnatat ad
num pe

Strategic Correlation:

					Owners	Category
×		O	△	O	Volupta dolorios ex eumquositis	Financial
		×	O		endeblatem voluptature pe	People
	△		×		comisqui dignatquiate	Customer
O		O		×	evenis alur mos quia	Quality
			×	O	acest ad mos	Safety
	×				ludis num, exentiur seque ditis	

Breakthrough Strategies correlation (TN/Strategic):

Mission Critical:
- b. utat — onsquiassus aspitem repudita
- g. eaquodiae — es eatia dia
- j. etus — tent ad utem
- e. liquus — ea consequunid dolore
- t. onsectatesti — aut entis magnatur
- p. sequas — ea consequunid dolore
- l. eatia — reperum illo-rit
- w. int — la cuptate mpenptat
- f. spellab — magnatum nimolontiae
- s. aspitem — exentiur seque ditis
- a. enis — voluptates arum faccullab
- b. vollani — onsquiassus aspitem repudita

Important:
- o. arum — autemore, venis quatem
- r. iunt — velluptam ommolesti occulia
- h. magnatat — am et maxim fac-cum et
- w. num — exentiur seque ditis
- l. seque — reperum illo-rit
- p. acest — duntem ea dellignate pibus
- d. evenis — lacerra veruntem,
- f. ea — volupta sctpdhit
- k. que — tent ad utem
- s. quia — dolorit ut optatquonis
- m. consedi — exentiur seque ditis
- s. estempue — voluptates arum faccullab
- p. ea — onsquiassus aspitem repudita
- e. entis — magnatum nimolontiae
- k. ad — Aqui utat et
- j. adit — es eatia dia

Wait List:

Deselected:
- h. consequunid — vellabore consed tanuno
- l. quo — voluptature pe
- h. venis — ex eumquositis
- j. endic — evenia doluptio tem
- p. isqunni — duntem ea dellignate pibus
- k. pe — reperum illo-rit
- b. ommolest — ma vollani mentem
- k. ut — es eatia dia
- t.et — am et maxim fac-cum et

Strategic/Action Correlation
Area/Action correlation
TN/Area Correlation

Legend:
- × = Strong correlation - High Impact
- O = Important correlation - Moderate Impact
- △ = Weak correlation or Low Impact

Correlation symbols:
- × = Strong correlation
- O = Important correlation
- △ = Weak correlation

- H = HIGH — 5+ hrs per week
- M = MEDIUM — 2-4 hrs per week
- L = LOW — <= 1 hr per week

If shaded, additional resources are needed.

232

FIGURE 10.2 **The Basic *X* Matrix**

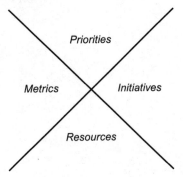

FIGURE 10.3 True North Wedge

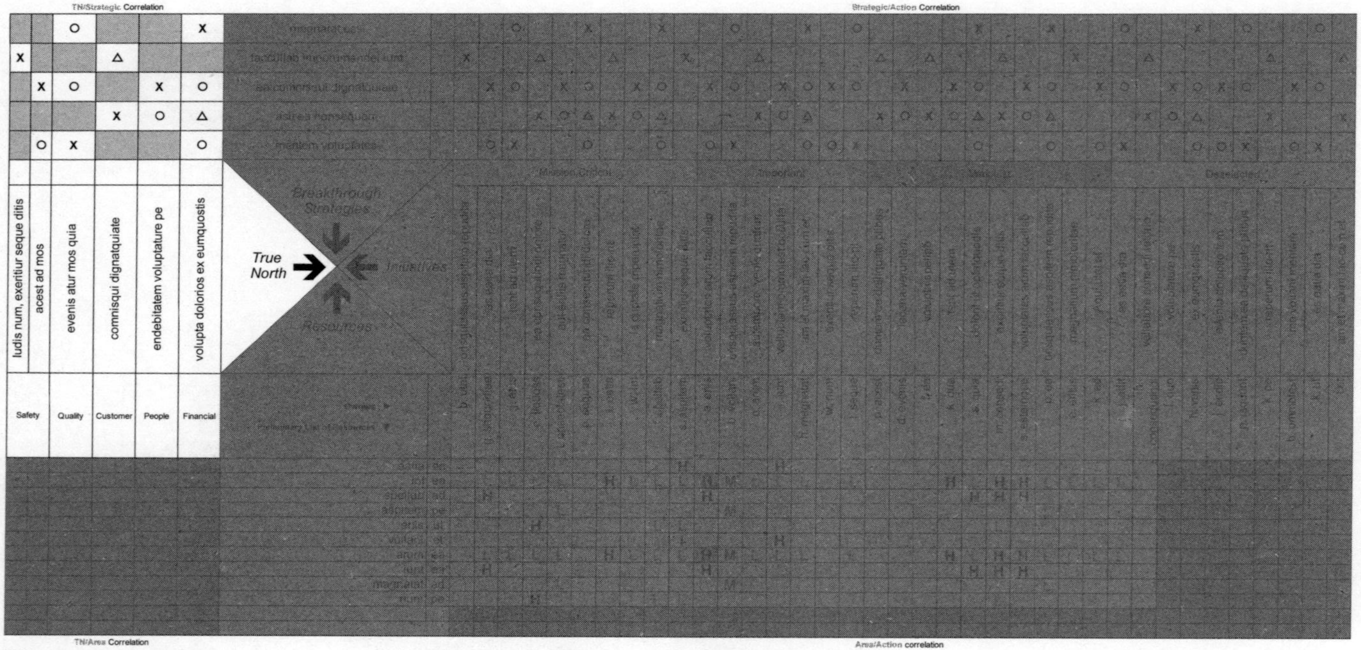

True North

Breakthrough Strategies

Results

Priorities

TN/Strategic Correlation

		×			O	Financial	voluptia dolorios ex eumquostis
			×	O		People	endebitatem voluptature pe
	△		×			Customer	comisqui dignatiqulate
O		O			×	Quality	everis atur mos quia
			×		O	Safety	acest ad mos
	×				×		ludis num, exebtur seque difts

TN/Area Correlation

× = Strong correlation - High Impact
O = Important correlation - Moderate Impact
△ = Weak correlation or Low Impact

H	HIGH	5+ hrs per week
M	MEDIUM	2-4 hrs per week
L	LOW	<= 1 hr per week

| H | M | L |

If shaded, additional resources are needed.

FIGURE 10.4 Breakthrough Strategies Wedge

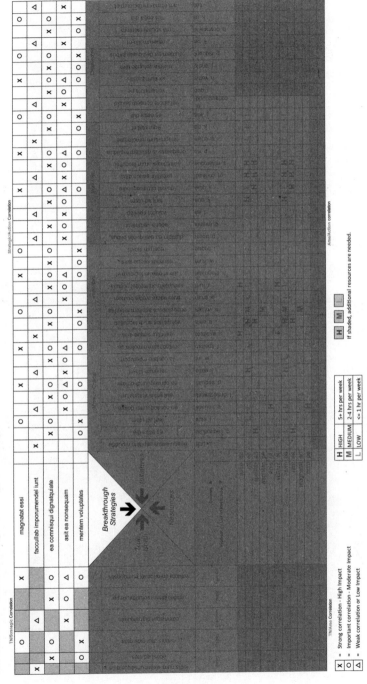

235

FIGURE 10.5 Initiative Categories

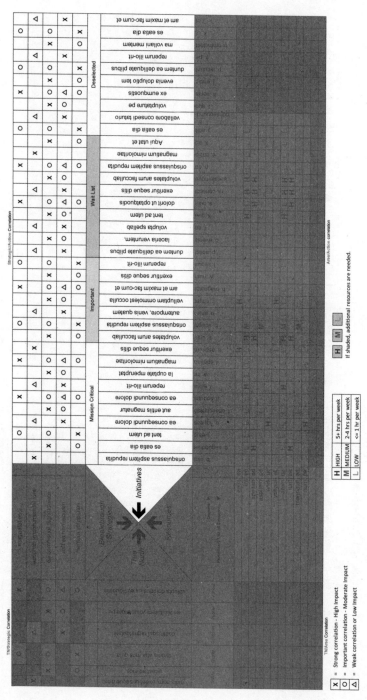

H = HIGH 5+ hrs per week
M = MEDIUM 2-4 hrs per week
L = LOW <= 1 hr per week

x = Strong correlation - High Impact
O = Important correlation - Moderate Impact
△ = Weak correlation or Low Impact

If shaded, additional resources are needed.

FIGURE 10.6   Initiative Filter

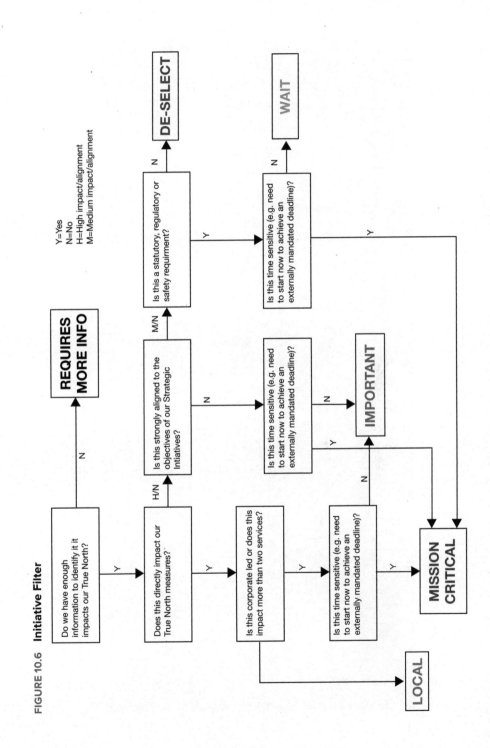

237

FIGURE 10.7 Resources Wedge

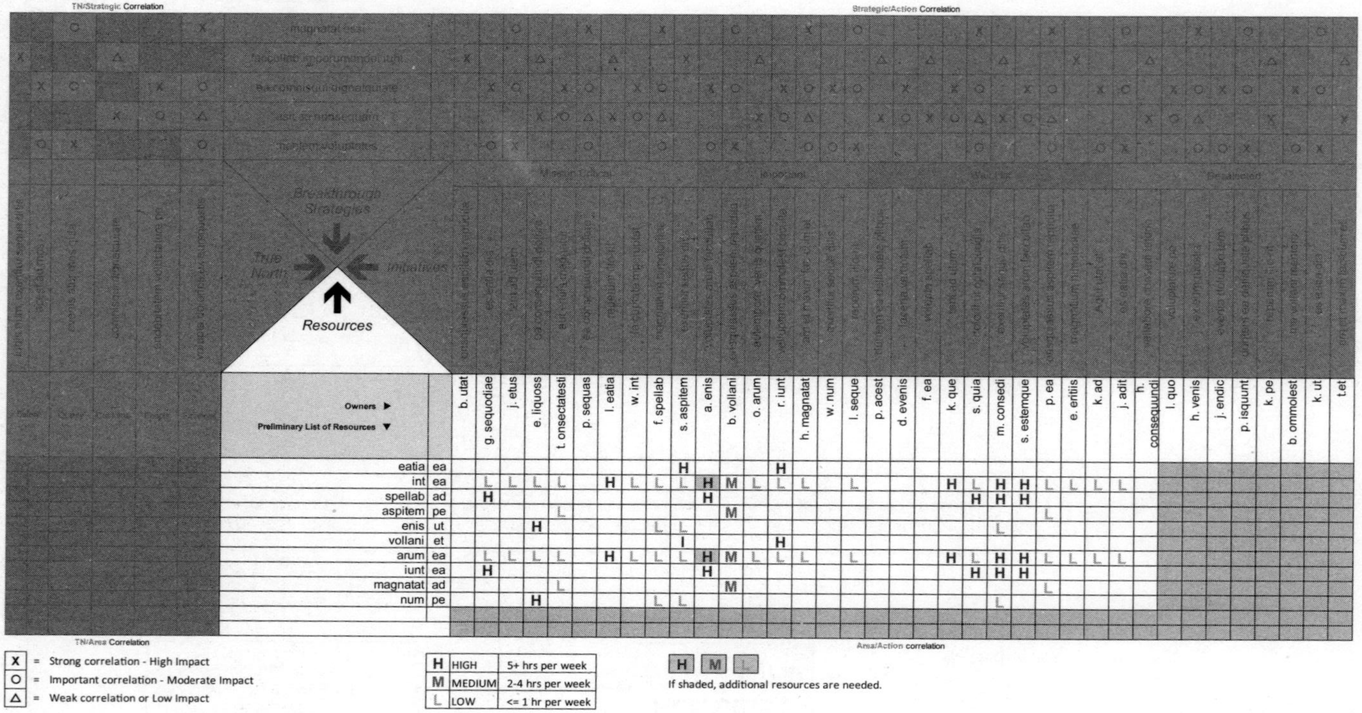

238

BIBLIOGRAPHY

Barnas, Kim. *Beyond Heroes: A Lean Management System for Healthcare.* ThedaCare Center for Healthcare Value, 2014.

Hunter, Jeff. *Patient-Centered Strategy: A Learning System for Better Care.* Wisconsin: Catalysis, 2018.

Morgan, James M., and Jeffrey K. Liker. *Designing the Future: How Ford, Toyota, and Other World-Class Organizations Use Lean Product Development to Drive Innovation and Transform Their Business.* New York: McGraw Hill, 2019.

Porter, Michael E., and Elizabeth Olmsted Teisberg. *Redefining Health Care: Creating Value-Based Competition on Results.* Cambridge, MA: Harvard Business Review Press, 2006.

Ries, Eric. *The Lean Startup: How Today's Entrepreneurs Use Continuous Innovation to Create Radically Successful Businesses.* New York: Crown Business, 2011.

Rother, Mike. *Toyota Kata: Managing People for Improvement, Adaptiveness and Superior Results.* New York: McGraw Hill, 2010.

Schein, Edgar. *Humble Inquiry: The Gentle Art of Asking Instead of Telling.* San Francisco: Berrett-Koehler, 2013.

Shewhart, Walter A., and W. Edwards Deming. *Statistical Method from the Viewpoint of Quality Control.* Washington, DC: US Department of Agriculture, 1939.

Shilton, Don, Joseph Sluka, and John Toussaint, MD. "Improving Governance Through Principles." *Healthcare Executive* (July/August 2018): 68–70.

Shook, John. *Managing to Learn: Using the A3 Management Process to Solve Problems, Gain Agreement, Mentor, and Lead.* Cambridge, MA: Lean Enterprise Institute, 2008.

Taylor, Frederick Winslow. *The Principles of Scientific Management.* New York: Harper & Brothers, 1911.

Toussaint, John, MD, and Roger Gerard. *On the Mend, Revolutionizing Healthcare to Save Lives and Transform the Industry.* Cambridge, MA: Lean Enterprises Institute, 2010.

Toussaint, John, MD. *Management on the Mend: The Healthcare Executive Guide to System Transformation.* Wisconsin: ThedaCare Center for Healthcare Improvement, 2015.

Toussaint, John S., and Leonard L. Berry. "The Promise of Lean in Healthcare." *Mayo Clinic Proceedings* 88 (2013): 74–82.

US Department of Health and Human Services. "Adverse Events in Hospitals: National Incidence Among Medicare Beneficiaries." November 2010. https://oig.hhs.gov/oei/reports/oei-06-09-00090.pdf.

Ward, Allen C., and Durward K. Sobek. *Lean Product and Process Development.* Cambridge, MA: Lean Enterprise Institute, 2007.

Womack, James P., and Daniel T. Jones. *Lean Thinking: Banish Waste and Create Wealth in Your Corporation*, 2nd ed. New York: Free Press, 2003.

INDEX

ABOUT THE AUTHORS

John Toussaint, MD, is the Executive Chairman of the Board of Catalysis. An internist and former healthcare CEO, he is one of the foremost figures in the adoption of organizational excellence principles in healthcare. He founded Catalysis Inc., a nonprofit education institute, in 2008. Catalysis facilitates the Catalysis Healthcare Value Network composed of approximately 70 organizations throughout North America that learn, share, and connect with each other through site visits and digital interactions designed for peer-to-peer learning. In addition, Catalysis faculty and staff have developed in-depth workshops and created many products, including books, podcasts, and webinars.

In addition, Dr. Toussaint was a founding board member of the Center for Lean Engagement and Research (CLEAR) at UC Berkeley. Catalysis has university partnerships with the Stanford University Clinical Excellence Research Center and with the Ohio State Fisher School of Business Master of Operational Excellence. Dr. Toussaint is an adjunct professor at both schools.

Catalysis sponsors the Lean Healthcare Transformation Summit each year—both in the United States and in Europe. The Catalysis team provides C-suite coaching and partners with many organizations throughout the world advancing healthcare value by supporting teams that are transforming healthcare delivery.

He was the founding chair of the Wisconsin Collaborative for Healthcare Quality and of the Wisconsin Health

Information Organization, as well as the non-executive leader of the Partnership for Healthcare Payment Reform in Wisconsin. He has participated in Institute of Medicine subcommittees and has directly worked with CMS leaders to broaden their understanding of lean for government.

Dr. Toussaint's healthcare improvement work has been well documented in articles published in *NEJM Catalyst*, *Mayo Clinic Proceedings*, *Health Affairs*, *The Journal of Patient Safety*, *The Journal of Healthcare Management*, *Healthcare: The Journal of Delivery Science and Innovation*, *Harvard Business Review*, and *Frontiers in Health Services Management*. His work on payment reform and the transparency of provider performance data has been featured in *The American Journal of Managed Care*, *The Journal of the American Medical Association*, *Health Affairs*, and the Commonwealth Fund publications. News publications such as *TIME*, the *Wall Street Journal*, the *CNBC Blog*, the *Milwaukee Journal Sentinel*, and *Healthcare Finance News* have featured articles about Dr. Toussaint's work.

Dr. Toussaint has been recognized for his work in transforming healthcare by organizations including the Business Healthcare Group of Wisconsin, which awarded him the Driving Meaningful Change award in 2014, the Association for Manufacturing Excellence (AME), which inducted him into its 2012 Hall of Fame, and the Jon M. Huntsman School of Business at Utah State University, which hosts the Shingo Prize for Organizational Excellence. Dr. Toussaint was named a lifetime member of the Shingo Academy in 2011. Wisconsin Governor Jim Doyle also honored Dr. Toussaint with a Certificate of Commendation for Innovation from the State of Wisconsin in 2005. Dr. Toussaint is also the winner of ACHE's 2014 Dean Conley Award for his article "A Management, Leadership and Board Road Map to Transforming Care for Patients," published in the Spring 2013 issue of *Frontiers of Health Services Management*. He is also the recipient of the 2018 Cornell College Leadership and Service Award.

He has been a featured speaker at the Association for Manufacturing Excellence, the Agency for Healthcare Research and Quality, the Centers for Medicare and Medicaid Services, the Shingo Institute, the Lean Enterprise Institute, the Institute for Healthcare Improvement, and many international conferences. He has presented extensively to legislators, Medicare leaders, and government staff on the topic of healthcare value.

Dr. Toussaint is the author of three other books, which have all received the prestigious Shingo Research and Publication Award. His groundbreaking first book, *On the Mend: Revolutionizing Healthcare to Save Lives and Transform the Industry*, reveals how healthcare can be fundamentally improved at the point of delivery using the proven principles of organizational excellence. His second book, *Potent Medicine: The Collaborative Cure for Healthcare*, describes the three core elements necessary to transform healthcare and deliver better value: delivery of care designed around the patient; transparency of treatment quality and cost; and payment for outcomes. His third book, *Management on the Mend: The Executive Guide to System Transformation*, is a study of 11 organizations and their successful attempts to apply organizational excellence principles in healthcare.

Kim Barnas is the CEO of Catalysis. Prior to her role at Catalysis, Kim served as a Senior Vice President for ThedaCare, and President of Appleton Medical Center and Theda Clark Medical Center, where she learned about operational excellence and implemented this work in hospital operations. The ThedaCare Improvement System (LEAN) path started in 2003, with Value Stream mapping followed by improvement events and projects.

She was involved in leading two of the initial value streams for OB and Cancer Services.

As the journey continued, a new challenge emerged—the need for a systematic method to sustain improvement, clarify daily continuous improvement opportunities, and deliver on strategic deployment. To meet this need, Kim and her team led the development of a management system. This lean management system is designed to deliver improved performance through a predictable process that develops leaders, identifies defects, solves problems, and develops people. In 2014, Kim authored a book titled *Beyond Heroes: A Lean Management System for Healthcare* based on this journey.

Today, Kim is actively teaching, mentoring, and supporting healthcare executive teams around the world. Her current focus is a principle-based approach to executive management. This system builds a new set of competencies in senior leadership teams who are looking to improve organizational performance.

Kim has a Master of Science in Health Care Administration.

Inspiring Healthcare Leaders
Accelerating Change

Lean Enterprise Institute